D0924722

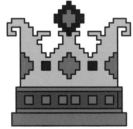
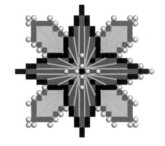

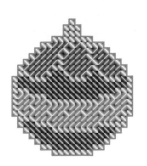

A Cross Stitcher's
COUNTDOWN TO CHRISTMAS

OVER 225 FESTIVE DESIGNS AND IDEAS

D&C
David and Charles

A DAVID & CHARLES BOOK
Copyright © David & Charles Limited 2008

David & Charles is an F+W Publications Inc. company
4700 East Galbraith Road, Cincinnati, OH 45236

First published in the UK & US in 2008

Text and designs copyright © Claire Crompton, Maria Diaz, Joan Elliott, Jane Henderson,
Ursula Michael, Joanne Sanderson, Lesley Teare and Shirley Toogood 2008
Photography, illustrations and layout copyright © David & Charles 2008

Claire Crompton, Maria Diaz, Joan Elliott, Jane Henderson, Ursula Michael, Joanne
Sanderson, Lesley Teare and Shirley Toogood have asserted their right to be identified as
authors of this work in accordance with the Copyright, Designs and Patents Act, 1988.

A catalogue record for this book is available from the British Library.

ISBN-13: 978-0-7153-2811-8 hardback
ISBN-10: 0-7153-2811-5 hardback

ISBN-13: 978-0-7153-2807-1 paperback
ISBN-10: 0-7153-2807-7 paperback

Printed in China by SNP Leefung PTE Ltd
for David & Charles
Brunel House   Newton Abbot   Devon

Senior Commissioning Editor: Cheryl Brown
Desk Editor: Bethany Dymond
Project Editor and Chart Preparation: Lin Clements
Senior Designer: Charly Bailey
Production Controller: Ros Napper
Photography: Kim Sayer, Anna Thompson and Karl Adamson

Visit our website at www.davidandcharles.co.uk

David & Charles books are available from all good bookshops; alternatively you can
contact our Orderline on 0870 9908222 or write to us at FREEPOST EX2 110, D&C Direct,
Newton Abbot, TQ12 4ZZ (no stamp required UK only); US customers call 800-289-0963
and Canadian customers call 800-840-5220.

Contents

Start the Countdown. . .

Christmas is an exciting time of year for most of us and the perfect excuse to get stitching. The wonderful designs in this book will allow you to create some eye-catching cards, beautifully crafted keepsakes and seasonal heirlooms to give to friends and family, or to display year after year in your own home.

That exciting run-up to Christmas is almost as enjoyable as the day itself, with all the planning and preparation that goes

into making the festival a fun time for everyone. But you don't have to cram all your stitching into those mad few weeks – why not savour the designs in this book and extend that delicious anticipation over the whole year?

For many children (and adults too!), the real excitement starts with an Advent calendar, and this book opens with a highly original Advent wall hanging – perfect to begin your leisurely countdown (or countup!) to Christmas. And by the time you get to 25, a beautiful nativity scene, you will be well and truly ready for the big day.

This book is a wonderful resource that you'll want to dip into again and again, with its fabulous collection of over 225 cross stitch motifs, providing you with all the designs and ideas you'll need to create a most memorable Christmas. The collection features the work of eight popular cross stitch designers, with designs ranging from classic to contemporary, humorous to traditional, and your fingers will soon be itching to create cards, gifts and decorations for the home. Each of the 25 chapters has clear colour charts, inspiring photographs and easy step-by-step stitching instructions.

A few hours of stitching is the perfect tonic after a busy day and will give you a real sense of achievement as you create lovely things to make the days of Christmas really special.

USING THIS BOOK

Many of the projects use cross stitch designs small enough to be made up in many different ways and you can follow the instructions to create the projects as shown in the photographs or choose a motif and make it up in another way of your choice.

It's easy to mix and match the designs – choose those you love and experiment with different ways of combining them. The motifs are also ideal for experimenting with different fabrics and threads.

There are suggestions throughout describing other ways to use the designs and ideas on embellishments you might use. Cross stitch designs can be partnered with many other art and craft materials.

Each chapter has its charted designs within the chapter, some of which have been made up into projects. Most of the charts have arrows indicating the centre of each motif and the stitch counts and finished design sizes. If in doubt refer to calculating design size on page 94.

The majority of making up instructions are at the back of the book beginning on page 96, and instructions on working the stitches are on page 95.

4

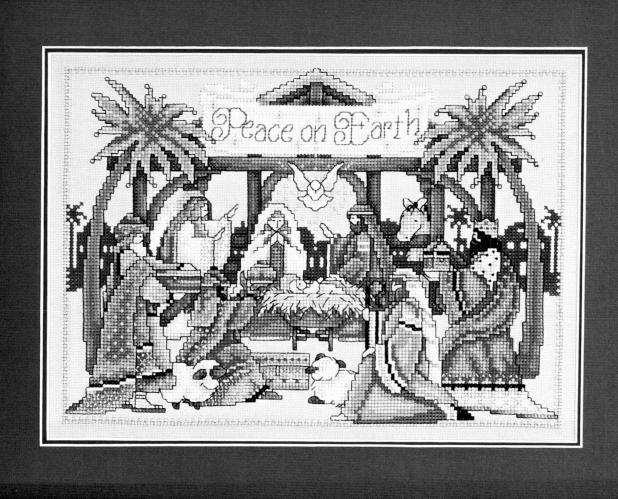

DESIGNED BY JOAN ELLIOTT

Advent Calendar

Count down the days until Christmas with this heirloom Advent calendar that you'll want to display for years to come. As anticipation grows, share the tradition of the season, turning over each of the 25 pillows to find a special Christmas motif on the other side, all of which are shown in the photo opposite. These tiny pillows are easy to assemble, with gold hangers and an edging of sparkling beads.

1 Prepare for work, referring to page 94 if necessary. Mark the centre of all the linen pieces and centre of the charted motifs. The picture motifs are stitched on either pale blue or putty linen – see diagram below. The number motifs are all stitched on platinum linen, with a backstitch box stitched in one of three different colours – see diagram.

2 To begin each motif, use backstitches over two fabric threads to stitch a square 21h x 21w for both the picture and number motifs 1–24, in the colours given in the diagram. Backstitch a rectangle 29h x 49w for both the picture and number for motif 25.

3 Sitch each picture motif over two fabric threads from the centre of the chart and centre of the backstitched box. Use one strand for Kreinik cross stitches and two strands for all other full and three-quarter cross stitches. Work French knots using two strands wound once around the needle. Use one strand for backstitches.

4 Stitch each number and its motif in the colours given in the chart. Before stitching numbers 11–25, plan them on graph paper.

5 Once all stitching is complete, see page 97 for making up the Advent calendar.

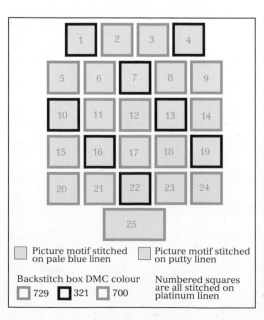

1	2	3	4
5	6	7	8	9
10	11	12	13	14
15	16	17	18	19
20	21	22	23	24
25			

☐ Picture motif stitched on pale blue linen ☐ Picture motif stitched on putty linen

Backstitch box DMC colour
☐ 729 ☐ 321 ☐ 700

Numbered squares are all stitched on platinum linen

Your Advent calendar will start the season on December 1 with all of the pillows showing their numbered sides. As the countdown to Christmas proceeds you will have the excitement of turning the pillows over to reveal the motif for the day.

YOU WILL NEED

Eleven 16.5cm (6½in) squares of light blue 28-count Jobelan, and one rectangle 17.8 x 21.6cm (7 x 8½in) – see diagram

✳

Thirteen 16.5cm (6½in) squares of putty 28-count Cashel linen (Zweigart code 3281/345/55) – see diagram

✳

Twenty-four 16.5cm (6½in) squares of platinum 28-count Cashel linen (Zweigart code 3281/770/55) and one rectangle 17.8 x 21.6cm (7 x 8½in)

✳

Tapestry needle size 24 and a beading needle

✳

DMC stranded cotton (floss) and Light Effects thread as listed in chart key

✳

Kreinik Fine #4 Braid 028 citron and Kreinik ⅛in ribbon 028 citron

✳

Mill Hill seed beads as listed in chart key

✳

Polyester filling for pillows

✳

Fabric for background 0.5m (½yd), and for border edging 0.25m (¼yd)

✳

Fusible fleece 0.5m (½yd)

✳

Twenty-five small star buttons and three large star buttons

✳

Dowel 40.6cm (16in) long, painted to tone with hanging

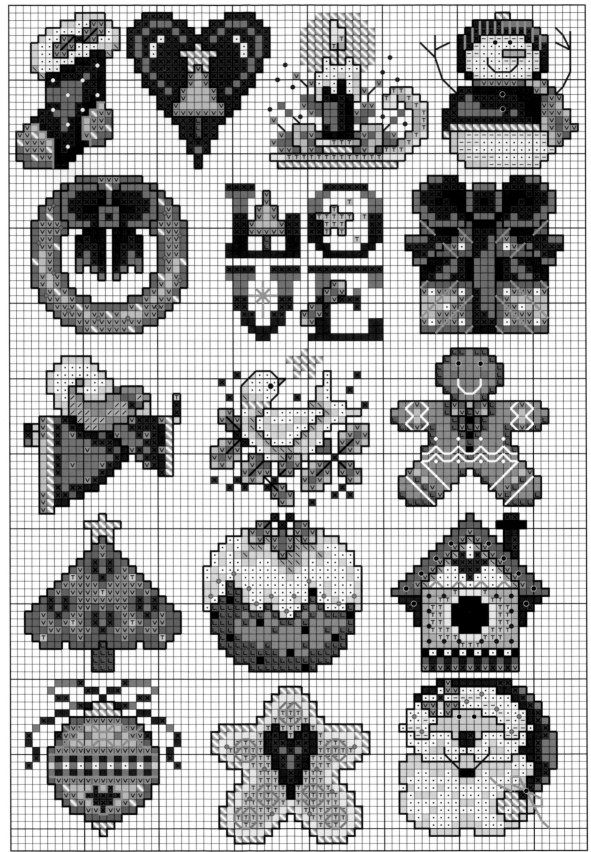

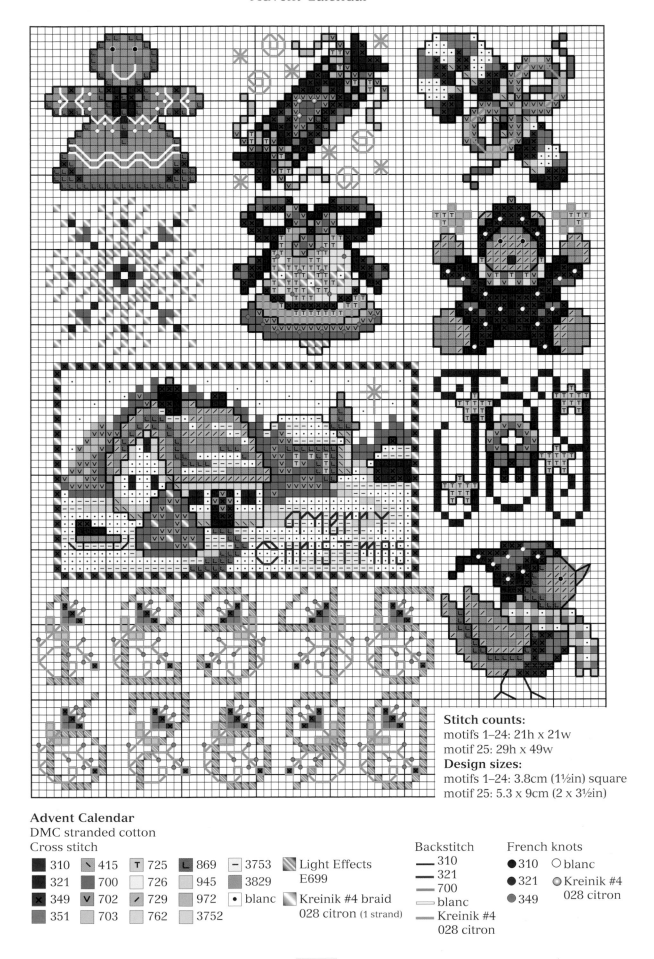

Stitch counts:
motifs 1–24: 21h x 21w
motif 25: 29h x 49w
Design sizes:
motifs 1–24: 3.8cm (1½in) square
motif 25: 5.3 x 9cm (2 x 3½in)

Advent Calendar
DMC stranded cotton
Cross stitch

■ 310	⬲ 415	T 725	L 869	– 3753	▨ Light Effects	
■ 321	▨ 700	726	945	3829	E699	
✕ 349	v 702	⁄ 729	972	• blanc	▨ Kreinik #4 braid	
■ 351	703	762	3752		028 citron (1 strand)	

Backstitch
— 310
— 321
— 700
▭ blanc
— Kreinik #4
  028 citron

French knots
● 310   ○ blanc
● 321   ◉ Kreinik #4
● 349   028 citron

DESIGNED BY LESLEY TEARE

CONE
YOU WILL NEED

Red or white 14-count
Aida 20.5cm (8in) square
❋
Tapestry needle size 26
❋
DMC stranded cotton
as listed in chart key
❋
Iron-on interfacing
❋
Permanent fabric glue
❋
Red bias binding
0.5m (½yd)

Scandinavian Christmas

These charming Scandinavian-inspired motifs are in traditional red and white and make striking decorations. The designs charted overleaf could be used for many projects, such as decorating table linen, adorning boxes or for Christmas cards. Here a snowflake design has been made up as a cone, which could be filled with sweets or a small gift. The heart makes a charming hanging for the Christmas tree.

HEART
YOU WILL NEED

Two pieces of red
14-count Aida
15cm (6in) square
❋
Tapestry needle size 26
❋
DMC stranded cotton
as listed in chart key
❋
Narrow red ribbon
15cm (6in) long
❋
Small red ribbon bow
❋
Small amount of stuffing
or pot-pourri

CONE

1 Prepare for work, referring to page 94 if necessary. Trace and cut out the cone template on page 102 and mark the outline in pencil on your Aida fabric. Mark the centre of the fabric and centre of the charted motif.

2 Start stitching from the centre of the fabric and the charted motif and work outwards over one Aida block using two strands of stranded cotton for cross stitch. Once the embroidery is complete, iron the interfacing on to the wrong side and refer to page 97 for making up the cone.

HEART

1 Prepare for work, referring to page 94 if necessary. Mark the centre of the fabric and the centre of the charted motif.

2 Start stitching from the centre of the fabric and the charted motif, working outwards over one Aida block using two strands of stranded cotton for cross stitch. Once all the stitching is complete, refer to page 98 for making up the heart.

DESIGNED BY JANE HENDERSON

Sweet Indulgence

Christmas is the perfect excuse to indulge your sweet tooth and the designs in this chapter are perfect for girly greetings, all featuring yummy motifs in the sweetest candy pink and chocolate shades. Some of the motifs use seed beads to bring an extra sparkle. The designs have been made up as Christmas cards but you could use them in other ways – see suggestions below. Stitch counts and design sizes are with the charts on pages 14 and 15.

YOU WILL NEED
(FOR ONE CARD)

White 14-count Aida
18cm (7in) square
❋
Tapestry needle size 26
and a beading needle
❋
DMC stranded cotton
(floss) as listed in
chart key
❋
Seed beads in pink or
gold (see charts)
❋
Double-sided
adhesive tape
❋
Single-fold card
to fit design

1 Prepare for work, referring to page 94 if necessary. Start stitching from the centre of the fabric and charted motif and work outwards over one Aida block using two strands of stranded cotton for cross stitch and French knots and one strand for backstitch. Where beads are used, attach them with a beading needle, matching thread and a half or full cross stitch.

2 Once the embroidery is complete, trim the fabric to within four or six rows of the embroidery and fray the edges by two rows all round. Using double-sided tape, stick the embroidery to the card and then embellish as desired.

You could stitch the smaller designs as gift tags, mounting the embroidery on to pretty card and decorating with glitzy embellishments. The scent bottles design would look wonderful edged with a thick braid and mounted on a metallic gold box in which you could store favourite perfumes.

Stitch counts: count the stitches across the height and the width of a motif and see page 94 for calculating finished design sizes

Heart template
(actual size)

Scandinavian Christmas
DMC stranded cotton
Cross stitch ■ 321

JANE HENDERSON

Sweet Indulgence
DMC stranded cotton

Cross stitch

		Backstitch	Seed beads
■ 632	■ 899	▬ 3731	— 154	● pink
■ 725	■ 963	O 3774	— 725	● gold
V 744	■ 3064	• blanc	— 801	
● 801	\ 3326			French knots
				● 154

Stitch counts and design sizes:

Baubles 35h x 36w	6.3 x 6.3cm (2½ x 2½in)
Hat boxes 39h x 24w	7 x 4.3cm (2¾ x 1¾in)
Bags and stars 61h x 26w	11 x 4.3cm (4½ x 1¾in)

Stitch counts and design sizes:

Perfume bottles	41h x 30w	7.5 x 5.5cm (3 x 2¼in)
Bag baubles	34h x 34w	6.3 x 6.3cm (2½ x 2½in)
Christmas tree	48h x 28w	9 x 5cm (3½ x 2in)
Gift for you	26h x 28w	4.3 x 5cm (1¾ x 2in)

DESIGNED BY CLAIRE CROMPTON

YOU WILL NEED

Antique blue 14-count Aida
40 x 35cm (16 x 14in)
※
Tapestry needle size 24
※
DMC stranded cotton
(floss) as listed in chart key
※
Thin wadding (batting)
※
Double-sided adhesive tape
※
Suitable picture frame

A Christmas Welcome

This utterly charming picture is sure to make family and friends feel most welcome in your home at Christmas time. It is stitched on a lovely antique blue Aida fabric, which provides a good contrast to all the bright colours. You could frame the design as a picture, as shown right, or make it up as a wall hanging and use a folk-art hanger to display it.

1 Prepare for work, referring to page 94 if necessary. Start stitching from the centre of the fabric and the chart overleaf and work outwards over one Aida block using two strands of stranded cotton for cross stitch.

2 Once all the stitching is complete, mount the design and frame it as a picture (see page 96) or make up in some other way of your choice – see suggestions below.

The Christmas Welcome design could be made up as a jolly cushion instead of a picture. The design also has lots of smaller motifs that could be used for other projects. For example, the two small houses could be stitched for Christmas cards, as could the little trees. If you are short on time the centre house could be worked as a small picture, perhaps with the word 'Welcome' stitched above it. The row of mittens could be stitched on Aida band, repeated three or four times to create a wonderful cake band for a Christmas cake or a fruit-topped Dundee cake.

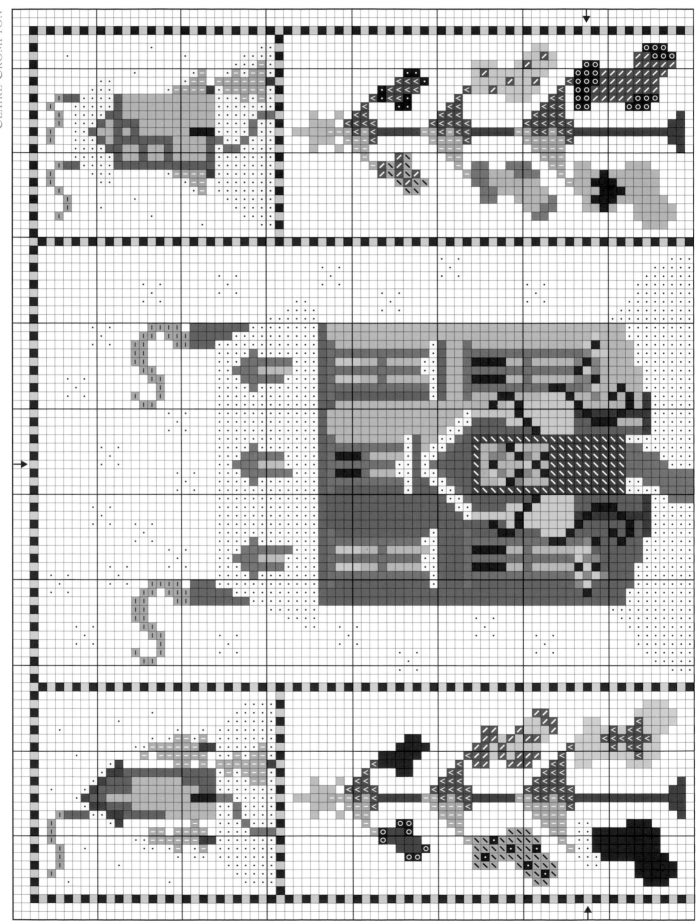

Stitch count: 131h x 103w
Design size: 23.5 x 18.5cm (9¼ x 7¼in)

A Christmas Welcome
DMC stranded cotton

Cross stitch

/ 153	/ 792	☑ 907	/ 3806	
– 159	◄ 904	931	3821	
321	905	3042	· blanc	
433	– 906	3752		
⊙ 550				
552				
740				
· 791				

DESIGNED BY JOAN ELLIOTT

Santa's Post Bag

Just like all of us, Santa is rushing to the post box with last-minute greetings. With help from a sweet teddy and two cheerful robins he manages to get his chores done in time for Christmas Day. This jolly post bag is big enough to hold all the season's correspondence: hang it in your hall, filled with post ready to send to friends and family. Decorated with metallic threads and shimmering beads the bag is sure to add an extra helping of Christmas cheer to your festive decorations.

1 Prepare for work, referring to page 94 if necessary. Find and mark the centre of the fabric and the centre of the chart overleaf. Mount your fabric in an embroidery frame if you wish.

2 Start stitching from the centre of the chart, using two strands of stranded cotton (floss) for full and three-quarter cross stitches. Use one strand to stitch all Kreinik #4 braid

cross stitches and backstitches. Work all other backstitches with one strand. Following the chart for colour changes, work French knots using one strand wrapped twice around the needle. Using a beading needle and matching thread, attach the beads (see page 95).

3 Once all the stitching is complete, finish your picture by making up into a post bag as described on page 98.

YOU WILL NEED

14-count antique white
Aida 33 x 38cm (13 x 15in)
✳
Tapestry needle size 24
and a beading needle
✳
DMC stranded cotton
(floss) as listed in
chart key
✳
Kreinik #4 braid as listed
in chart key
✳
Mill Hill seed beads
02054 brilliant shamrock
and 03049 rich red
✳
Backing fabric 0.5m (½yd)
✳
Heavyweight iron-on
interfacing and fusible
fleece 0.5m (½yd) each
✳
Decorative trim 2m (2yd)
✳
Three decorative buttons
✳
Permanent fabric glue
✳
Dowel painted to
tone with embroidery
33cm (13in) long

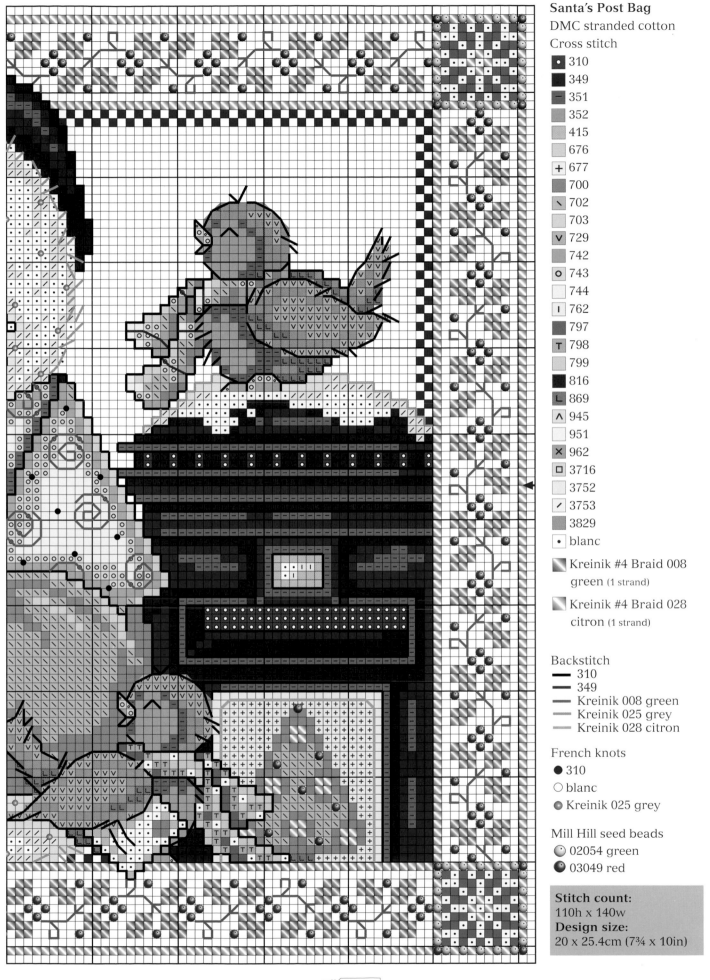

Santa's Post Bag
DMC stranded cotton

Cross stitch

- 310
- 349
- 351
- 352
- 415
- 676
- 677 (+)
- 700
- 702 (\)
- 703
- 729 (v)
- 742
- 743 (o)
- 744
- 762 (I)
- 797
- 798 (T)
- 799
- 816
- 869 (L)
- 945 (^)
- 951
- 962 (×)
- 3716 (□)
- 3752
- 3753 (/)
- 3829
- blanc (•)

Kreinik #4 Braid 008 green (1 strand)

Kreinik #4 Braid 028 citron (1 strand)

Backstitch
- 310
- 349
- Kreinik 008 green
- Kreinik 025 grey
- Kreinik 028 citron

French knots
- 310
- blanc
- Kreinik 025 grey

Mill Hill seed beads
- 02054 green
- 03049 red

Stitch count:
110h x 140w
Design size:
20 x 25.4cm (7¾ x 10in)

23

DESIGNED BY LESLEY TEARE

Winter Garden

Six delightful designs celebrate the flora and fauna that can be seen during the winter months. The three birds are the robin, blue tit and wren, while the floral designs are poinsettia, Christmas rose and a traditional wreath. The designs have been made up as attractive scented sachets that will bring a festive fragrance to your house. Stitch counts and design sizes are with the charts overleaf.

1 Prepare for work, referring to page 94 if necessary. Mark the centre of the fabric and centre of the charted motif. Mount your fabric in an embroidery frame if you wish.

2 Start stitching from the centre of the fabric and the centre of the chart. Work over one Aida block using two strands of stranded cotton or Light Effects thread for cross stitches and then one strand for backstitches.

3 The flower designs are embellished with seed beads. Attach beads with half cross stitching, a beading needle and matching thread (see page 95).

4 Once your embroidery is complete, check for missed stitches and then make up the sachet in one of the two ways described on page 98.

YOU WILL NEED
(FOR ONE SACHET)

White 16-count Aida 15cm (6in) square
✳
Tapestry needle size 26 and a beading needle
✳
DMC stranded cotton and Light Effects thread as listed in chart key
✳
Mill Hill seed beads 00557 gold and 00165 red (see charts)
✳
Backing fabric to tone with embroidery
✳
Thin gold ribbon 23cm (9in) long
✳
Two small bells or a gold tassel
✳
Pot-pourri (or some polyester stuffing)

You can make your sachets up to hang in two different ways – either on point with a tassel at the bottom, as the Christmas Rose sachet here shows, or straight with little bells in the corners, as for the robin sachet.

DESIGNED BY JOAN ELLIOTT

Mantel Stocking

You can't have Christmas without cheerful stockings to fill with sweets and trinkets. Surprise everyone in the family on Christmas morning with these festive stocking ornaments hanging on your tree. There are five designs to choose from and the stockings would also make charming party gifts for guests. Petite jingle bells added along each band bring a special touch of Christmas. See the charts on page 28 for stitch counts and design sizes.

1 Prepare for work, referring to page 94 if necessary. Mark the centre of the fabric and centre of the charted motif.

2 Start stitching from the centre of the chart and centre of the Aida band and work outwards over one block. Use two strands of stranded cotton for cross stitches but one strand of Kreinik thread. Work French knots using two strands wound once around the needle. Use one strand for all backstitches and long stitches. Use two strands of blending filament to overstitch Santa's beard and hat fur in half cross stitches. Using a beading needle and matching thread, attach the seed beads (see page 95).

3 Once stitching is complete, see page 99 for making up into a decoration. A full size template is given on page 29.

YOU WILL NEED
(FOR ONE DECORATION)

White/red 16-count Aida band (Zweigart code 7107/019) 17.5cm (7in)
❄
Tapestry needle size 24 and a beading needle
❄
DMC stranded cotton (floss) as listed in chart key
❄
Kreinik Fine #4 Braid 028 citron and Blending Filament 032 pearl
❄
Mill Hill seed beads 00557 gold and 03049 rich red
❄
Two pieces of patterned fabric 25.4 x 17.8cm (10 x 7in)
❄
Decorative trim 50.8cm (20in) long and thin ribbon for hanging
❄
Five decorative jingle bells
❄
Iron-on interfacing
❄
Permanent fabric glue

Robin

Blue Tit

LESLEY TEARE

Wren

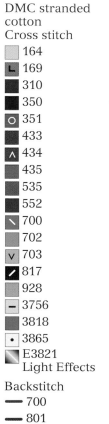

Stitch counts (each design): 54h x 54w
Design sizes: 8.5cm (3³⁄₈in) square

Robin
DMC stranded cotton
Cross stitch

	164
L	169
	310
	350
O	351
	433
∧	434
	435
	535
	552
\	700
	702
V	703
/	817
	928
−	3756
	3818
•	3865
/	E3821 Light Effects

Backstitch
— 700
— 801

Blue Tit
DMC stranded cotton
Cross stitch

	310
	435
\	700
	702
U	726
	727
+	734
×	793
/	817
	928
	3012
−	3756
	3807
	3818
•	3865
/	E3821 Light Effects

Backstitch
— 310
— 700
— 801

Wren
DMC stranded cotton
Cross stitch

	164
	310
O	351
	433
∧	434
	435
\	437
	535
	552
V	703
I	712
	739
/	817
−	3756
	3818
•	3865
/	E3821 Light Effects

Backstitch
— 700
— 801

Poinsettia

Christmas Rose

Wreath

Poinsettia
DMC stranded cotton
Cross stitch
- 164
- ◉ 350
- 351
- 552
- 702
- ⋁ 703
- ⟍ 772
- ■ 817
- Ⅰ 3756
- • 3865
- ◩ E3821 Light Effects

Backstitch
- — 700
- — 801

Mill Hill seed beads
- ◯ 00557 gold

Christmas Rose
DMC stranded cotton
Cross stitch
- 164
- ◉ 350
- 552
- ✕ 700
- 702
- ⟍ 772
- 3818
- • 3865
- ◩ E3821 Light Effects

Backstitch
- — 700
- — 801

Mill Hill seed beads
- ◯ 00557 gold

Wreath
DMC stranded cotton
Cross stitch
- ✕ 700
- 702
- ■ 817
- 3807
- 3818
- • 3865
- ◩ E3821 Light Effects

Backstitch
- — 700
- — 801

Mill Hill seed beads
- ⬤ 00165 red

Stitch counts (each design): 54h x 54w
Design sizes: 8.5cm (3³/₈in) square

Mantel Stocking

DMC stranded cotton

Cross stitch

■	310
■	321
■	349
■	351
■	415
■	700
╱	702
■	703
■	725
□	726
■	797
◣	798
■	799
■	869
■	945
V	972
L	3829
•	blanc
▨	Kreinik #4 braid 028 citron (1 strand)

Backstitch

— 310
— 700
— Kreinik #4 braid 028 citron

French knots

● 310
● 321
● 349

Mill Hill seed beads

◉ 00557 gold
◎ 03049 rich red

Use two strands of Kreinik Blending Filament 032 and half cross stitch over Santa's beard and hat fur

Stitch count (each design): 24h x 39w
Design size: 3.8 x 6.2cm (1½ x 2½in)

JOAN ELLIOTT

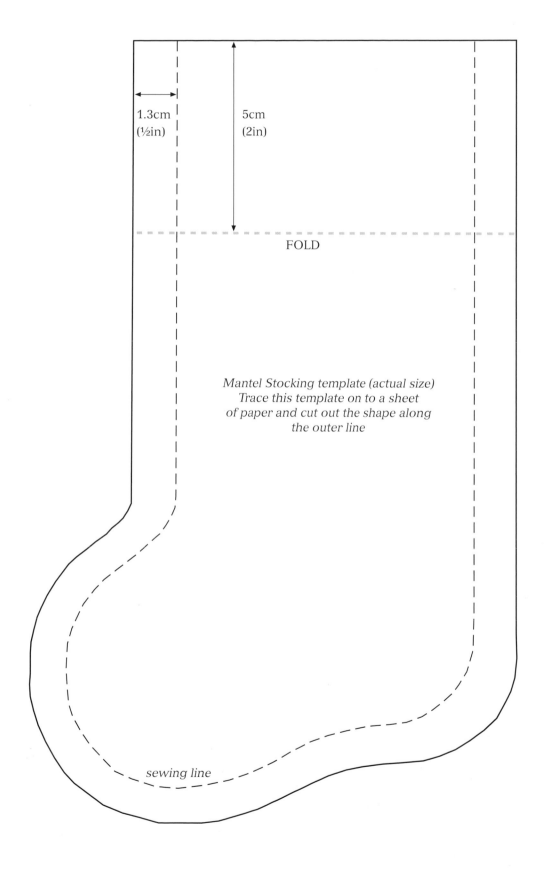

1.3cm
(½in)

5cm
(2in)

FOLD

Mantel Stocking template (actual size)
Trace this template on to a sheet
of paper and cut out the shape along
the outer line

sewing line

DESIGNED BY URSULA MICHAEL

Mittens Garland

Ajingle bells and mittens garland makes a delightful project and this lovely blue and white garland can be enjoyed throughout the winter. A traditional red and green version has also been charted on page 33 and is perfect for Christmas time. The instructions are for the blue and white mittens: if stitching the alternate version choose different coloured ribbons to tone. Instead of a garland, you could stitch up all eight designs and use them for Christmas cards.

1 Prepare for work, referring to page 94 if necessary. Mark the centre of the fabric and the centre of the charted motif. Stitch counts and design sizes for each mitten are with the charts overleaf.

2 Start stitching from the centre of the fabric and chart and work outwards over one Aida block using two strands of stranded cotton for cross stitch and one for

backstitch. Use one strand when using the Kreinik metallic thread. Use a beading needle and matching thread to attach the seed beads in the positions shown on the chart. If you prefer, you could work French knots instead of using beads.

3 When stitching is complete, stitch the other three designs and make up as a garland as described on page 99.

YOU WILL NEED
(FOR FOUR MITTENS)

Four pieces of white 14-count Aida 15.2cm (6in) square
❊
Tapestry needle size 26
❊
DMC stranded cotton as listed in chart key
❊
Kreinik Fine #4 Braid 001 silver
❊
Mill Hill seed beads as listed in chart key
❊
Four pieces of backing fabric 15.2cm (6in) square
❊
Silver ribbon 150cm (60in) long x 1.3cm (½in) wide
❊
Blue ribbon 150cm (60in) long x 2.5cm (1in) wide (optional)
❊
Eight small silver bells
❊
Polyester stuffing

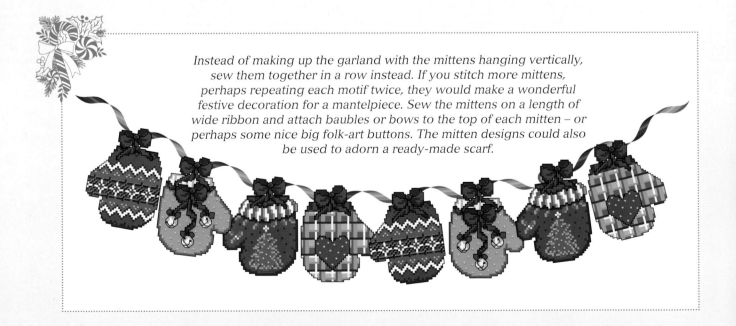

Instead of making up the garland with the mittens hanging vertically, sew them together in a row instead. If you stitch more mittens, perhaps repeating each motif twice, they would make a wonderful festive decoration for a mantelpiece. Sew the mittens on a length of wide ribbon and attach baubles or bows to the top of each mitten – or perhaps some nice big folk-art buttons. The mitten designs could also be used to adorn a ready-made scarf.

Blue and White Mittens
DMC stranded cotton
Cross stitch

▫	799	•	blanc
▨	798	◩	Kreinik #4 braid
▪	796		001 silver
			(1 strand)

Backstitch
— 820
— Kreinik #4
001 silver

Mill Hill seed beads
◉ 02010 silver
◔ 02058 white
◉ 02064 turquoise

Stitch counts (each design):
40h x 37w
Design sizes:
7 x 6.7cm (2¾ x 2½in)

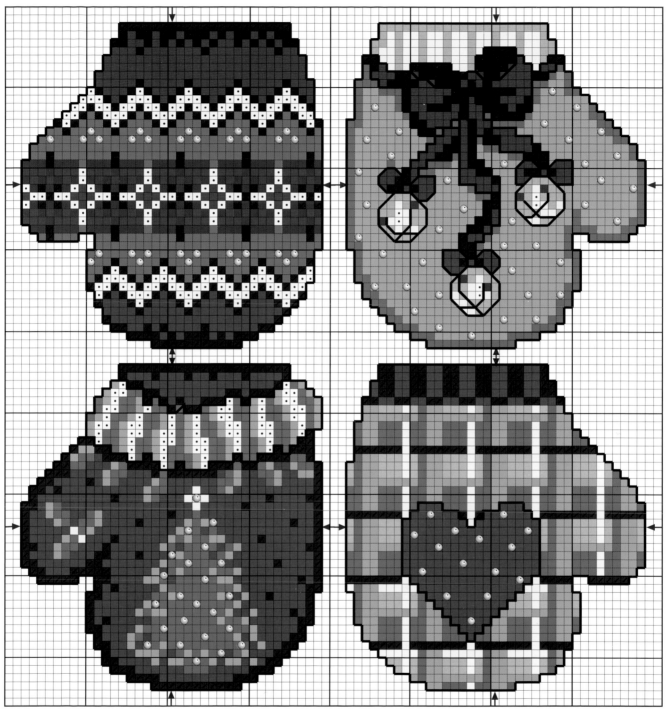

Red and Green Mittens
DMC stranded cotton
Cross stitch

				Backstitch	Mill Hill seed beads
■ 310	□ 726	▨ 3820		— 310	◉ 03041 pearl
■ 321	◩ 816	⊡ blanc			
▨ 702	■ 986				

DESIGNED BY LESLEY TEARE

YOU WILL NEED

White 14-count Aida
20.3cm (8in) square
for design shown
❅
Tapestry needle size 26
❅
DMC Light Effects
threads and stranded
cotton (floss) as listed
in chart key
❅
Double-sided adhesive
film (from craft shops)
❅
Sturdy box 15.3cm (6in)
square or to fit
your design
❅
Wide ribbon 1m (1yd)
for a bow

Luxury Bauble Box

Use these sumptuous, sparkling motifs to decorate a sturdy box in which to store your most precious tree decorations. Stitch the design shown opposite or choose from the borders and motifs charted overleaf to make up your own designs (see some ideas below). The cross stitches are worked in beautiful metallic threads and the simple backstitching in gold or black adds simple details. See page 94 for calculating stitch counts and finished design sizes.

1 Prepare for work referring to page 94 if necessary. Mark the centre of the fabric and the centre of the chart. Mount your fabric in an embroidery frame if you wish.

2 Start stitching from the centre of the fabric and centre of the chart and work outwards over one Aida block. Use two strands of thread for cross stitches and one strand for backstitches. Use shorter lengths of metallic threads – about 30.5cm (12in).

3 Once the embroidery is complete, cut a piece of double-sided adhesive film slightly bigger than the embroidery. Peel the protective sheet from the front of the adhesive and stick it to the back of the embroidery. Trim to size and then peel away the backing sheet from the adhesive film and place the embroidery in position on your box. Press down firmly. To finish, tie a decorative ribbon around the box and form a bow.

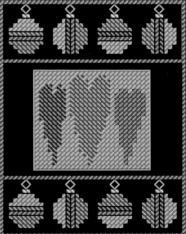

The sparkly motifs in this chapter are very adaptable: they can be used for many projects and can also be combined in various ways to create a pattern of your own design. Experiment with stitching them on bolder fabric colours too, to create more dramatic effect, such as the black and rich blue shown here.

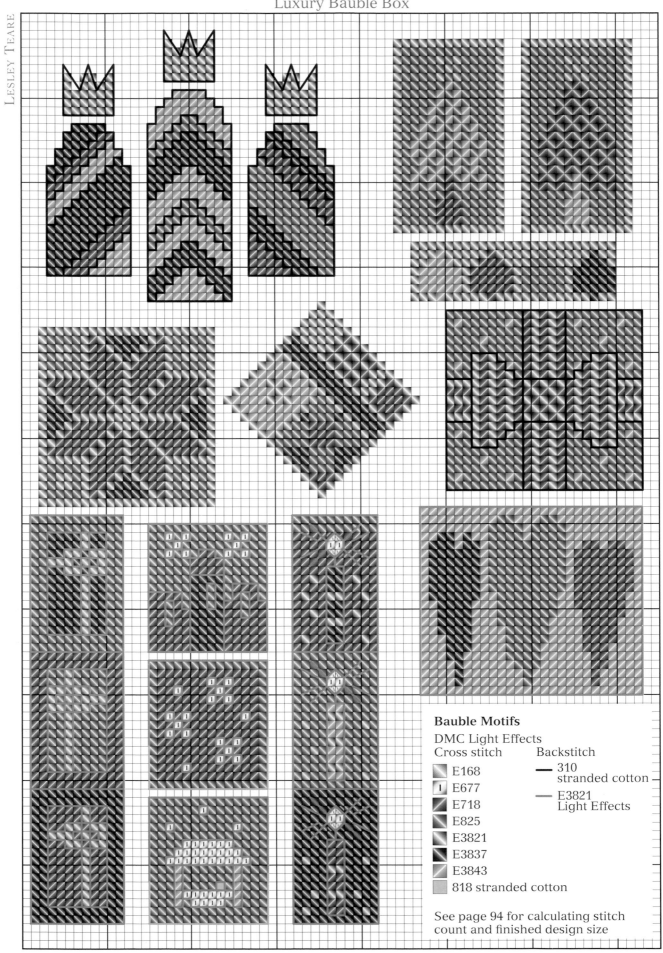

Bauble Motifs

DMC Light Effects

Cross stitch		Backstitch	
	E168	—	310 stranded cotton
I	E677	—	E3821 Light Effects
	E718		
	E825		
	E3821		
	E3837		
	E3843		
	818 stranded cotton		

See page 94 for calculating stitch count and finished design size

DESIGNED BY URSULA MICHAEL

Gingerbread Gift Tags

These charming handmade gift tags double as keepsake ornaments when the paper tag backing is removed. Some delicious cookie motifs (charted on page 41) would also make wonderful tags or cards or could be used to decorate Christmas table linen or an apron for the hard-working cook.

1 Prepare for work, referring to page 94 if necessary. Start stitching from the centre of the fabric and charted motif overleaf and work outwards over one Aida block using two strands of stranded cotton for cross stitch and one strand for backstitch.

2 Once stitching is complete, iron fusible adhesive on to the wrong side of the stitching according to the manufacturer's instructions. Peel the paper backing from the adhesive and iron on the backing fabric. Trim excess fabric from around the stitched area.

3 Make up the tag as follows. Cut a piece of yellow card about 3.8 x 6.3cm (1½ x 2½in), using pinking shears or deckle-edged scissors. Cut a piece of red card into a tag shape large enough to house the gingerbread motif and the yellow card. Use tacky glue to stick the piece of yellow card on to the bottom of the tag.

4 Use tacky glue to stick the gingerbread motif to the red card, slipping a scrap of narrow, folded ribbon for a hanger behind the embroidery before pressing down. Finish by writing your own message on the yellow card.

Christmas Greetings!

Just for you xxx

December

11

DESIGNED BY MARIA DIAZ

YOU WILL NEED
(FOR EACH DESIGN)

White 16-count Aida
20cm (8in) square

❄

Tapestry needle size 26

❄

DMC stranded cotton and
metallic thread as listed in
chart key

❄

Double-fold card with
aperture to fit embroidery

❄

Decorative panel for card
(see Suppliers)

❄

Double-sided tape

❄

Embellishments
as desired

Greetings from Teddy

Six exuberant teddies will make the most wonderful set of Christmas cards. The card mounts have been given extra festive colour with decorative panels in a contrasting shade. You could also stitch these cute teddies on 14-count Aida and use them for other projects, such as little pictures or placemats for the Christmas table. If stitched on 16-count Aida, the designs will fit a card with a 10cm (4in) square aperture. See the charts on pages 42 and 43 for stitch counts and design sizes.

1 Prepare for work, referring to page 94 if necessary. Start stitching from the centre of the fabric and charted motif and work outwards over one Aida block using two strands of stranded cotton for cross stitch and one strand for backstitch.

2 Place the decorative panel diagonally over the card aperture and stick each corner securely with double-sided tape. Turn the card over and carefully cut out the centre of the panel. Mount the embroidery into the card as described on page 96 and embellish further if desired.

Gingerbreads
DMC stranded cotton
Cross stitch

			Backstitch
321	436	986	—— 321
350	437	3371	—— 3371
434	701	• blanc	

Stitch counts: 47h x 37w maximum
Design sizes: 8.5 x 6.7cm (3⅜ x 2¾in) max

40

Cookies
DMC stranded cotton
Cross stitch

			Backstitch
● 321	▨ 436	▨ 986	— 321
350	437	■ 3371	— 3371
434	701	● blanc	

Stitch counts: 45h x 38w maximum
Design sizes: 8.2 x 6.7cm (3¼ x 2¾in) max

MARIA DIAZ

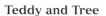

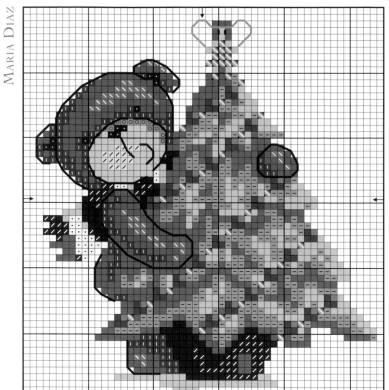

Teddy and Tree
DMC stranded cotton
Cross stitch

					Backstitch
◪ 351	552	762	— 989	O 3821	— 3781
352	554	817	I 869	• blanc	— 5284
420	744	I 869	3346		metallic
◩ 436	◪ 746	951	3348	◪ 5284 metallic	
				3781	

Stitch count: 57h x 52w
Design size: 9 x 8.2cm (3½ x 3¼in)

Teddy and Stocking
DMC stranded cotton
Cross stitch

					Backstitch
◪ 351	552	762	3346	• blanc	— 3781
352	554	817	3348		
420	744	I 869	3781		
◩ 436	◪ 746	— 989	O 3821		

Stitch count: 49h x 45w
Design size: 7.6 x 7.2cm (3 x 2⅞in)

Teddy Carol Singing
DMC stranded cotton
Cross stitch

				Backstitch
420	744	I 869	O 3821	— 3781
◩ 436	◪ 746	— 989	• blanc	
552	762	3346		
554	817	3781		

Stitch count: 54h x 46w
Design size: 8.4 x 7.3cm (3⅜ x 2⅝in)

Teddy and Presents
DMC stranded cotton
Cross stitch

				Backstitch
✓ 351	554	■ 817	▪ 3781	— 3781
420	744	❙ 869	○ 3821	
＼ 436	／ 746	— 989	◣ 5284	
552	762	3346	metallic	

Stitch count: 51h x 58w
Design size: 8 x 9.2cm (3$^{1}/_{8}$ x 3$^{5}/_{8}$in)

Teddy and Pudding
DMC stranded cotton
Cross stitch

				Backstitch
✓ 351	554	■ 817	▪ 3781	— 3781
420	744	❙ 869	○ 3821	
＼ 436	／ 746	— 989	• blanc	
552	762	3346		

Stitch count: 49h x 45w
Design size: 7.6 x 7.2cm (3 x 2$^{7}/_{8}$in)

Teddy Skating
DMC stranded cotton
Cross stitch

				Backstitch
✓ 351	／ 746	— 989	◣ 5284	— 3781
420	762	3346	metallic	
＼ 436	■ 817	▪ 3781		
744	❙ 869	○ 3821		

Stitch count: 53h x 48w
Design size: 8.4 x 7.6cm (3$^{3}/_{8}$ x 3in)

DESIGNED BY SHIRLEY TOOGOOD

Beaded Decorations

These gorgeous decorations studded with shiny seed beads will bring a brilliant sparkle to your Christmas preparations. If you're feeling creative and want to make a really luxurious decoration you could substitute the beaded tassel for an inexpensive crystal jewellery pendant, available from many high-street stores. The designs charted overleaf would also be wonderful for cards and gift tags.

1 Prepare for work, referring to page 94 if necessary. Start stitching from the centre of the fabric and charted motif (charts overleaf) and work outwards over one Aida block using two strands of stranded cotton or Light Effects thread for cross stitch. Use one strand of Light Effects thread for backstitch or long stitch. Attach the beads in the positions shown on the chart using a beading needle, matching thread and cross stitch.

2 Once all the stitching is complete, make up the design as a card or gift tag or refer to page 99 for making up as a tree decoration.

These attractive designs can be used in many other ways and you can have great fun rearranging them – perhaps to stand 'on point' in a group of four as shown below left. Try stitching them on different coloured fabrics, perhaps as a sparkly patch on a diary cover or ready-made gift bag. You could also change the colours to other striking combinations, such as red and pewter or the emerald and copper example shown below right.

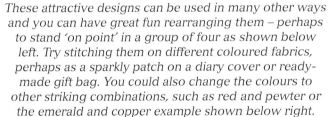

YOU WILL NEED
(FOR ONE DECORATION)

White 14-count Aida
10.2cm (4in) square

❈

Tapestry needle size 24
and a beading needle

❈

DMC stranded cotton and
Light Effects thread as
listed in chart key

❈

Seed beads in gold or
silver (see charts)

❈

Selection of decorative
beads and sequins

❈

Thick wadding (batting)

❈

Backing fabric 10.2cm
(4in) square

❈

Narrow gold ribbon

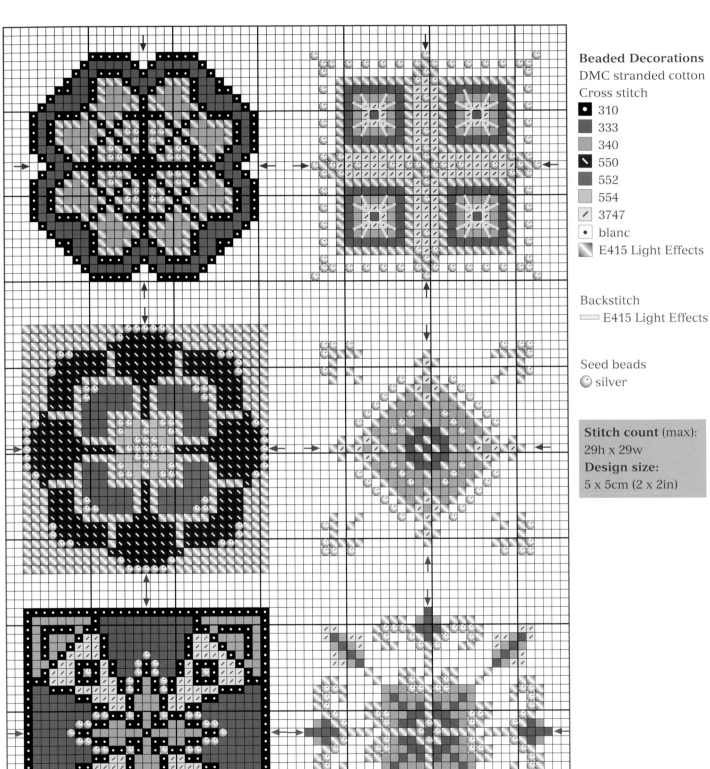

Beaded Decorations
DMC stranded cotton
Cross stitch

- ◨ 310
- ▩ 333
- ▨ 340
- ◩ 550
- ▩ 552
- ▨ 554
- ◹ 3747
- • blanc
- ▨ E415 Light Effects

Backstitch
▭ E415 Light Effects

Seed beads
◯ silver

Stitch count (max):
29h x 29w
Design size:
5 x 5cm (2 x 2in)

SHIRLEY TOOGOOD

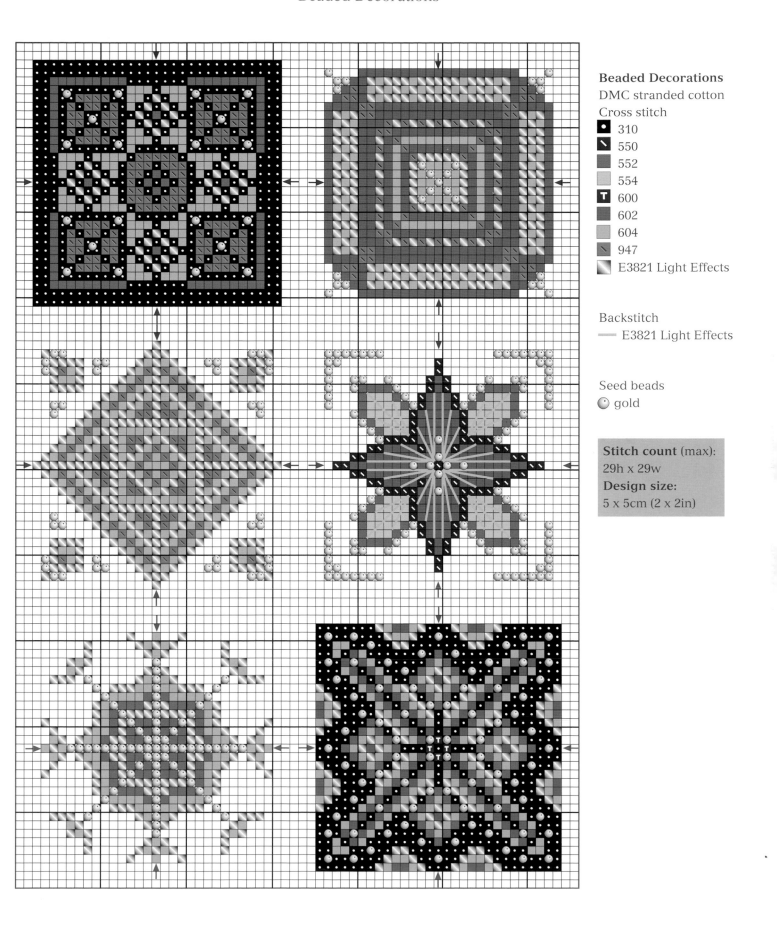

Beaded Decorations
DMC stranded cotton
Cross stitch

⬛	310
◣	550
⬛	552
⬜	554
T	600
⬛	602
⬜	604
◿	947
◨	E3821 Light Effects

Backstitch
— E3821 Light Effects

Seed beads
◐ gold

Stitch count (max):
29h x 29w
Design size:
5 x 5cm (2 x 2in)

DESIGNED BY SHIRLEY TOOGOOD

YOU WILL NEED
(FOR ONE TAG)

White 14-count Aida
10.2 x 9cm (4 x 3½in)
✳
Tapestry needle size 24 and
a beading needle
✳
DMC stranded cotton
(floss) as listed in chart key
✳
Seed beads in red, gold
and white
✳
Iron-on interfacing
✳
Coloured card
✳
Narrow gold ribbon and
gold rickrack braid
✳
Craft glue
✳
Hole punch

Christmas Wishes

The charming little designs used for these tags will bring your sincerest Christmas wishes to all your friends and family. The designs have a multitude of uses, for example, you could use them to decorate a little tree as seen opposite, perhaps placed as a focal point on a Christmas buffet table or in a hall to welcome guests into your home. The designs would also make a lovely collection of greetings cards for your favourite people.

1 Prepare for work, referring to page 94 if necessary. Start stitching from the centre of the fabric and charted motif (charts overleaf) and work outwards over one Aida block using two strands of stranded cotton for cross stitch and French knots and one strand for backstitch. Attach the beads using a beading needle, matching thread and half cross stitch.

2 Once the embroidery is complete, trim the fabric to within two rows of the stitching all round and fray the edge back one block. Trim thread ends carefully so they don't show when the interfacing is fused in place. Cut a

piece of interfacing to the shape of the tag and iron it on to the back of the stitching following the manufacturer's instructions.

3 To make a card tag first cut a piece of coloured card to a tag shape approximately 1.3cm (½in) bigger all round than the trimmed embroidery. Glue the stitching in the centre of the card tag. Decorate the tag by gluing a strip of narrow gold rickrack braid on the card below the stitching, or choose your own embellishments. Finish by punching a hole at the top of the card and looping a length of narrow gold ribbon through the hole for a tie.

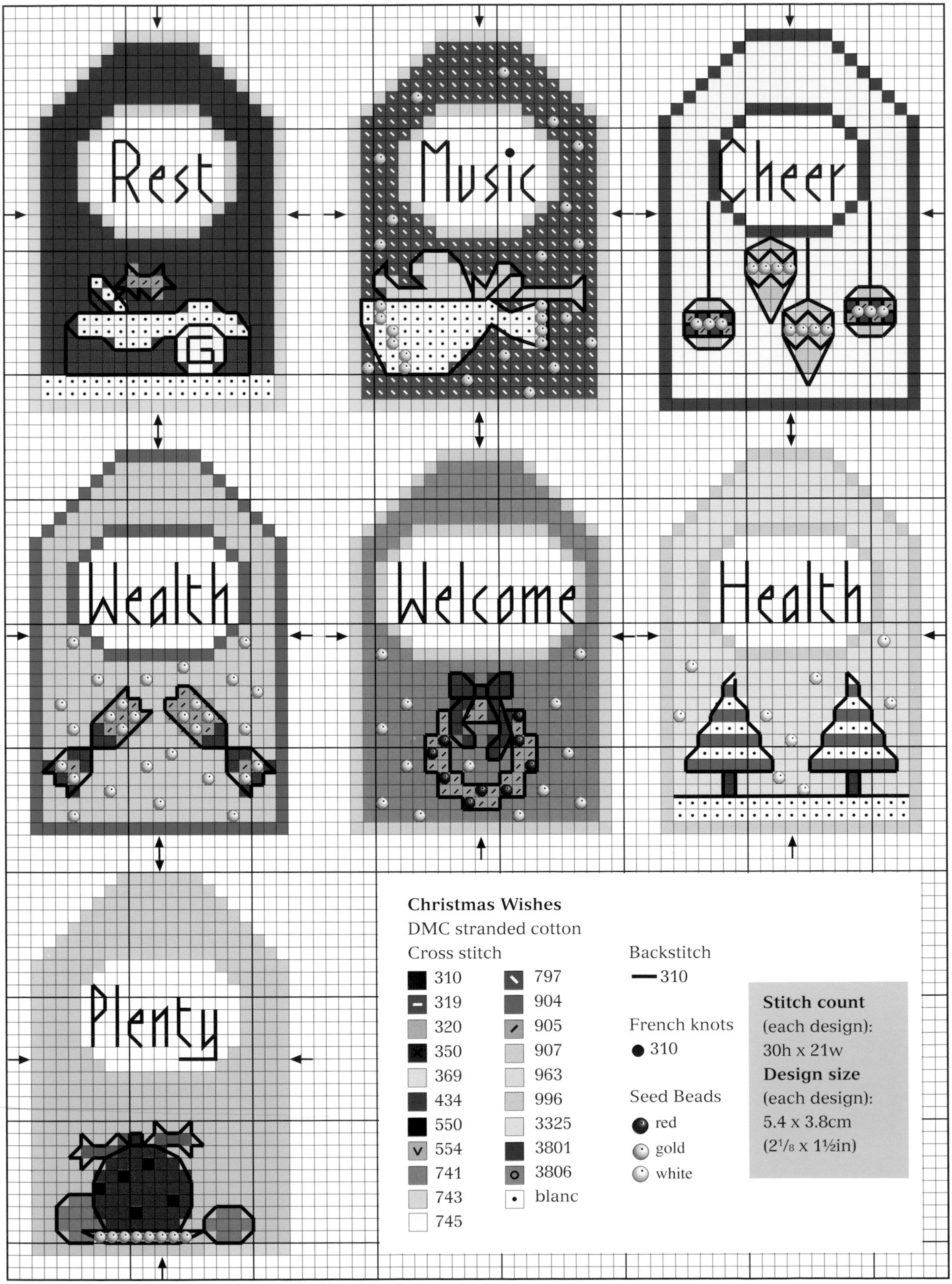

SHIRLEY TOOGOOD

Rest

Music

Cheer

Wealth

Welcome

Health

Plenty

Christmas Wishes
DMC stranded cotton
Cross stitch

■	310	◩	797
▬	319		904
	320	◪	905
▩	350		907
	369		963
	434		996
	550		3325
☑	554		3801
	741	⊙	3806
	743	•	blanc
	745		

Backstitch
— 310

French knots
● 310

Seed Beads
● red
◔ gold
○ white

Stitch count
(each design):
30h x 21w
Design size
(each design):
5.4 x 3.8cm
(2¹⁄₈ x 1½in)

50

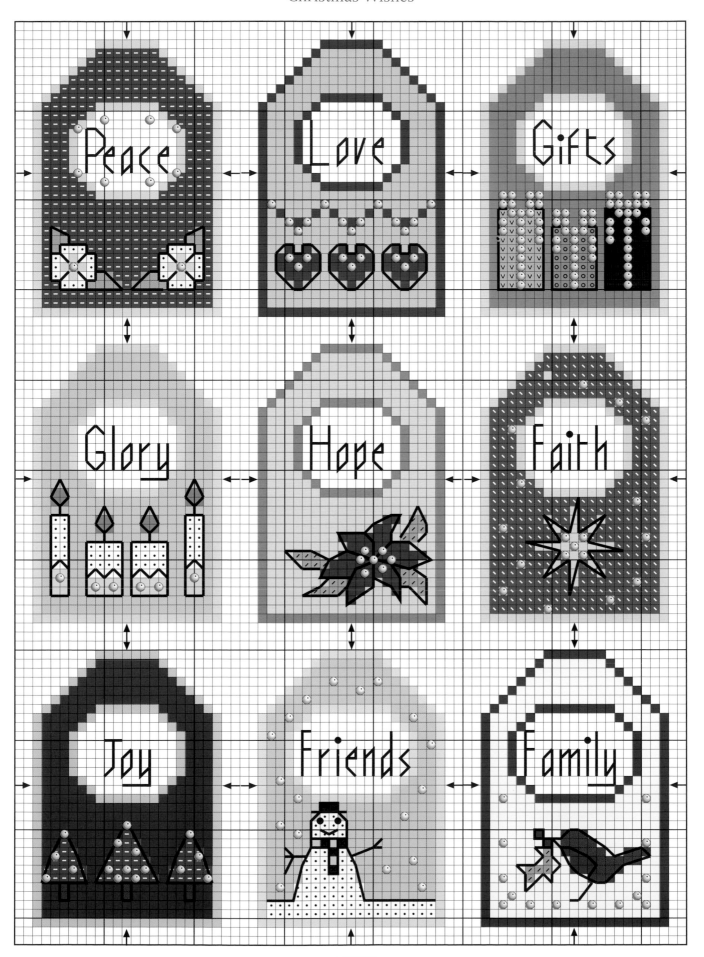

DESIGNED BY MARIA DIAZ

YOU WILL NEED

White 14-count Aida band
5cm (2in) wide x 50cm
(20in) long
✳
Tapestry needle size 26
✳
DMC stranded cotton and
metallic thread as listed in
chart key
✳
Small piece of hook and
loop tape (Velcro)

Traditional Treats

Two attractive band designs with a traditional look will allow you to decorate all sorts of gifts and embellish delicious treats for the Christmas table, such as the cake band shown here. Aida and linen bands are available in different colours and widths, with various decorative edgings, including silver and gold. If you prefer working on linen, you could also stitch either of these designs over two threads of 28-count linen band.

1 Begin by measuring the circumference of your cake and adding 1.3cm (½in) at either end for small hems – this will be the length you need to stitch the design. Start stitching from the centre of the fabric and the chart overleaf and work outwards over one Aida block using two strands of stranded cotton for cross stitch and one for backstitch. Repeat the design as often as necessary to the length you require.

2 When all stitching is complete, hem the ends of the band and stitch a square of Velcro to either end. Secure the band around your cake and admire.

Band designs are very versatile and can be used to decorate many objects – perfect for Christmas gifts. You could add an embroidered band to a jar of homemade cookies or a tin of luxury chocolates. Stitch up a shorter band to adorn jars of jams, pickles and chutneys ready for the Christmas feast. Embroidered bands can also be glued to the covers of journals and albums. Why not stitch the sleigh design on a dark green band with a gold edge and glue it to a sturdy box filled with a supply of Christmas cards? A single motif could also be used for a card or gift tag, adding a name or message using one of the alphabets on page 55.

DESIGNED BY SHIRLEY TOOGOOD

Festive Bands

Two beautifully adorned candles are shown here with designs so pretty you are sure to want to use them every year. Cross stitching designs on ready-made bands couldn't be simpler and you can use the designs to decorate Christmas gifts and seasonal keepsakes, to bring a special touch to the Christmas table and to give the whole house a charming, hand-crafted atmosphere.

YOU WILL NEED
(FOR ONE BAND)

White 14-count Aida band (see step 1)
✳
Tapestry needle size 24
✳
DMC stranded cotton (floss) as listed in chart key
✳
Iron-on interfacing
✳
White velvet ribbon 3mm (1/8in) wide
✳
Fast-tack craft glue

1 The band designs charted on pages 56–57 have various widths – see page 57 for the minimum width of band you will need for each design. To calculate the length of band needed, measure the circumference of the item to be decorated and cut your band to that length, plus another 2.5cm (1in) for turnings. Instead of a band, you could use a strip of embroidery fabric, as shown on the shorter candle below.

2 Start stitching from the centre of the band or fabric strip and the centre of the chart and work outwards over one Aida block using two strands of stranded cotton for cross stitch and French knots and one strand for backstitch and long stitch. Stitch the required number of repeats along the fabric.

3 If you have used Aida band, wrap your finished band around the candle, fold the ends over where they meet and slipstitch them together to hold the band on the candle.

If you have used a strip of fabric, trim the fabric to within four blocks of the stitching and glue lengths of narrow velvet ribbon along the top and bottom edges. Cut a strip of iron-on interfacing, fuse it to the back of the band and attach to the candle as above.

These attractive candle bands are for decoration only and should be removed before setting light to the candles. Never leave a burning candle unattended.

MARIA DIAZ

Traditional Treats

DMC stranded cotton
Cross stitch

								Backstitch
╱	210		553		913		3818	— 159
⊙	321	−	747		950	◩	5284 metallic	— 550
	351	◣	816		3740			— 5284 metallic
•	550	V	910	I	3746			

Stitch counts (each band): 26h x 155w
Design sizes: 4.7 x 28cm (1⁷⁄₈ x 11in)
Both bands can be repeated
to the length of your choice

Use the alphabets and numbers charted
opposite to create names messages and
personalize any of the designs in the book,
changing the backstitch to a colour your choice.

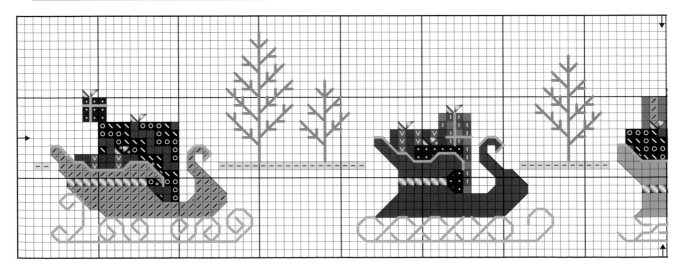

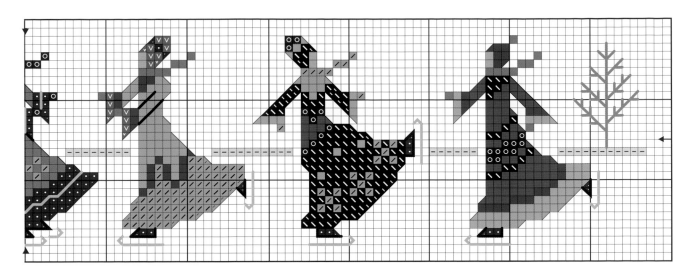

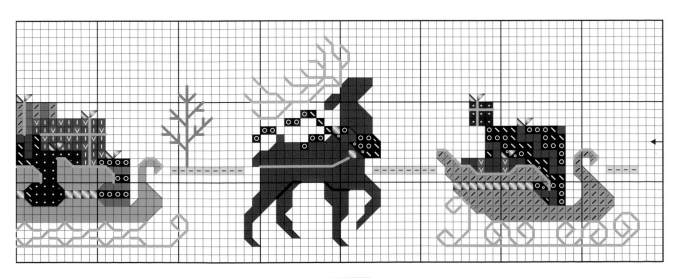

Festive Bands
DMC stranded cotton

Cross stitch

● 310	I 745	╱ 996	3818
434	✕ 817	L 3705	3846
743	○ 911	3801	· blanc

Backstitch
— 310
— 900
▭ blanc

French knots
○ blanc

The band designs are various widths and can be repeated to any length. See opposite for minimum band width required and refer to page 94 for calculating finished design sizes.

56

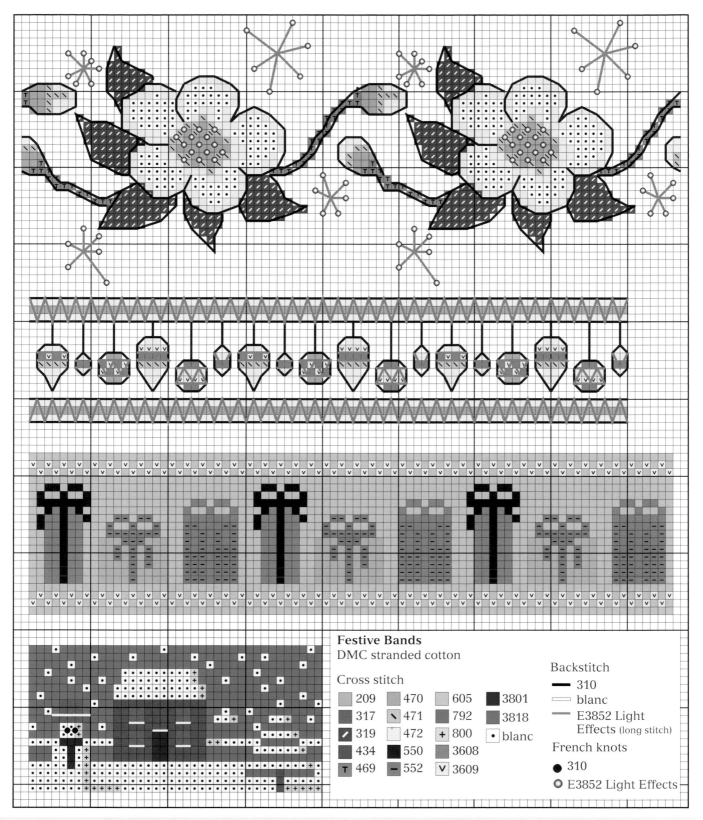

Festive Bands
DMC stranded cotton

Cross stitch

209	470	605	3801
317	\ 471	792	3818
◢ 319	472	+ 800	• blanc
434	550	3608	
T 469	− 552	V 3609	

Backstitch
— 310
▭ blanc
— E3852 Light
Effects (long stitch)

French knots
● 310
◎ E3852 Light Effects

Minimum band width required:

Crown: 24 stitches high, needs 5cm (2in) wide band
Garland: 27 stitches high, needs 6.3cm (2½in) wide band
Penguins: 25 stitches high, needs 5cm (2in) wide band
Gingerbread: 21 stitches high, needs 5cm (2in) wide band

Christmas rose: 34 stitches high, needs 7.6cm (3in) wide band
Baubles: 16 stitches high, needs 3.8cm (1½in) wide band
Parcels: 21 stitches high, needs 5cm (2in) wide band
Snowy house: 19 stitches high, needs 3.8cm (1½in) wide band

DESIGNED BY JOANNE SANDERSON

School Nativity

Watching children perform in a school nativity play is a delightful occasion for most parents and these adorable designs capture that sweet innocence perfectly, as well as reminding us of the true meaning of Christmas. The stitch count for the design shown as a decorative patch on a family photo album is 55 high x 60 wide, with a finished size of 10 x 11cm (4 x 4¼in).

1 Prepare for work, referring to page 94 if necessary. Start stitching from the centre of the fabric and charted motif (charts overleaf) and work outwards over one Aida block using two strands of stranded cotton for cross stitch and one for backstitch. Use a sharp needle to stitch the facial features and position the stitches accurately.

2 Using the alphabet charted, plan out the letters on graph paper before stitching. Alternatively, you could create different

wording – see some examples below. The alphabets on page 55 could also be used to create messages.

3 Trim the embroidery to 13cm (5in) square and stick it to the cardboard with double-sided tape. Using matching thread, stitch the blue cord all around the embroidery. Stick the mounted fabric on to the centre of the album and tie the cord ends into a bow. Loop the charm on to the silver cord and then tie it around the bow.

YOU WILL NEED

White 14-count Lurex
Aida 25cm (10in) square
❋
Tapestry needle size 24
❋
DMC stranded cotton
(floss) as listed in
chart key
❋
Photograph album
(see Suppliers)
❋
Dark blue cord 1m (1yd)
❋
Fine silver cord or thread
❋
Cardboard 13cm
(5in) square
❋
Double-sided
adhesive tape
❋
Metal bauble charm
(see Suppliers)

The motifs charted overleaf can be mixed and matched in many different ways to create all sorts of charming projects. You could make some lovely Christmas cards, such as the three kings shown here, using the alphabet to create messages. Embellish cards with Christmas-themed stick-ons. For a larger project you could stitch a Christmas banner featuring a row of the Nativity characters, which would be a beautiful keepsake to be displayed each year. Mount it on stiff card and glue on a jumbo ric-rac trim with star buttons on the corners.

School Nativity

DMC stranded cotton

Cross stitch

L	210		436		743		948
●	310	◢	498	T	745		995
	413		666		754		996
V	414		703		909		3746
	415	◥	739	▬	938	I	3838
	433	o	741		946		3840

● B5200

◪ E3821
Light Effects

Backstitch

— 310

— 498

— E3821 Light Effects

French knots

● 310

● 498

Stitch counts and design sizes:

Kings 35h x 37w

6.3 x 6.5cm (2½ x 2¾in)

Angel 37h x 22w

6.5 x 4cm (2½ x 1½in)

Animals 35h x 45w

6.3 x 8.2cm (2½ x 3¼in)

Mary and Joseph 35h x 28w

6.3 x 5cm (2½ x 2in)

Nativity scene
45h x 53w
8.2 x 9.6cm
(3¼ x 3¾in)
Shepherd
36h x 18w
6.5 x 3.2cm
(2½ x 1¼in)
Angel and Shepherds
38h x 67w
7 x 12cm
(2¾ x 4¾in)

DESIGNED BY CLAIRE CROMPTON

Gift Pillow

A sweet pillow with a special little pocket for a gift makes a lovely Christmas present. The one shown opposite would be perfect for a little girl (or even a grown-up one!), while the fun Santa and Rudolph version charted on page 65 is sure to be welcomed by any little boy. Some parts of the design are given an extra festive sparkle by the use of DMC Light Effects threads tweeded with the stranded cotton. Refer to the charts for stitch counts and finished sizes.

YOU WILL NEED
(FOR ONE PILLOW)

White 14-count Aida:
one 22cm (9in) square
for pillow patch and
one 14cm (5½in) square
for pocket

✳

Tapestry needle size 24

✳

DMC stranded cotton and
Light Effects thread as
listed in chart key

✳

Fabric for the pillow, two
24cm (9¾in) squares

✳

Lightweight iron-on
interfacing 22cm
(9in) square

✳

Polyester stuffing

1 For the pillow patch, mark the centre of the larger piece of Aida and the centre of the chart overleaf. Start stitching from the centre of the chart and fabric, working over one Aida block

2 Use two strands of stranded cotton for cross stitch and for French knots. Where stranded cotton and Light Effects thread are used together, use one strand of each together in the needle. For backstitch use the number of strands indicated in the chart key. Do not stitch the three stars in the tinted pocket box yet.

3 Use the alphabet to chart the name, centring it in the name box. Backstitch the name using two strands of red. For the pocket, work the three stars in the centre of the smaller Aida piece.

4 Once all stitching is complete, see page 100 for making up.

A gift pillow for a boy is easy to create using the chart on page 65. Why not be adventurous and use a different colour Aida for the pocket, perhaps matching it to your pillow fabric? There are lots of great Christmas fabrics to choose from and you could use shiny seed beads instead of French knots. If the name is a short one, you could add some hearts and kisses to help fill the space.

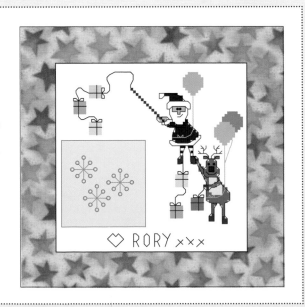

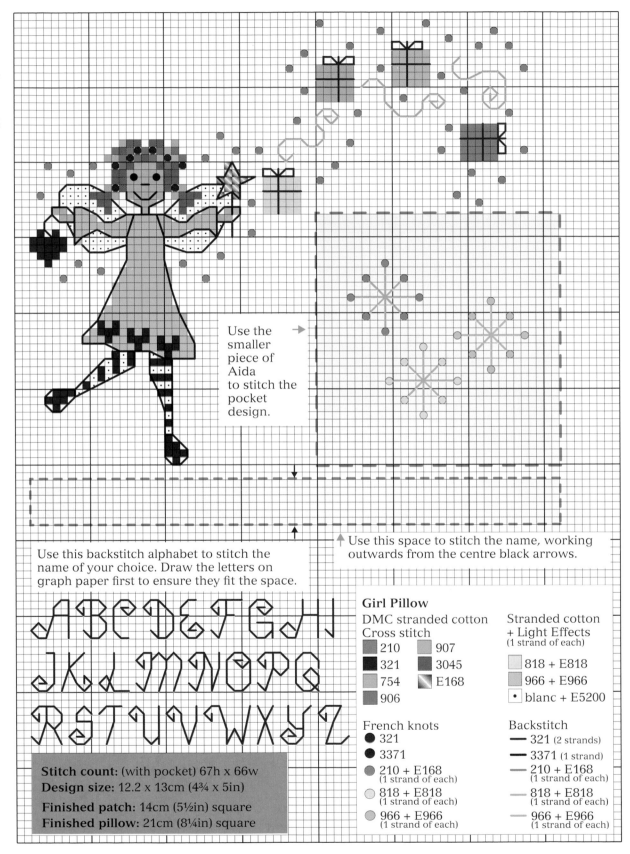

Use the smaller piece of Aida to stitch the pocket design.

↑ Use this space to stitch the name, working outwards from the centre black arrows.

Use this backstitch alphabet to stitch the name of your choice. Draw the letters on graph paper first to ensure they fit the space.

Girl Pillow

DMC stranded cotton
Cross stitch

▨ 210	▨ 907	
■ 321	▨ 3045	
▨ 754	◩ E168	
▨ 906		

Stranded cotton
+ Light Effects
(1 strand of each)

- ▨ 818 + E818
- ▨ 966 + E966
- • blanc + E5200

French knots
- ● 321
- ● 3371
- ● 210 + E168 (1 strand of each)
- ○ 818 + E818 (1 strand of each)
- ● 966 + E966 (1 strand of each)

Backstitch
- — 321 (2 strands)
- — 3371 (1 strand)
- — 210 + E168 (1 strand of each)
- — 818 + E818 (1 strand of each)
- — 966 + E966 (1 strand of each)

Stitch count: (with pocket) 67h x 66w
Design size: 12.2 x 13cm (4¾ x 5in)
Finished patch: 14cm (5½in) square
Finished pillow: 21cm (8¼in) square

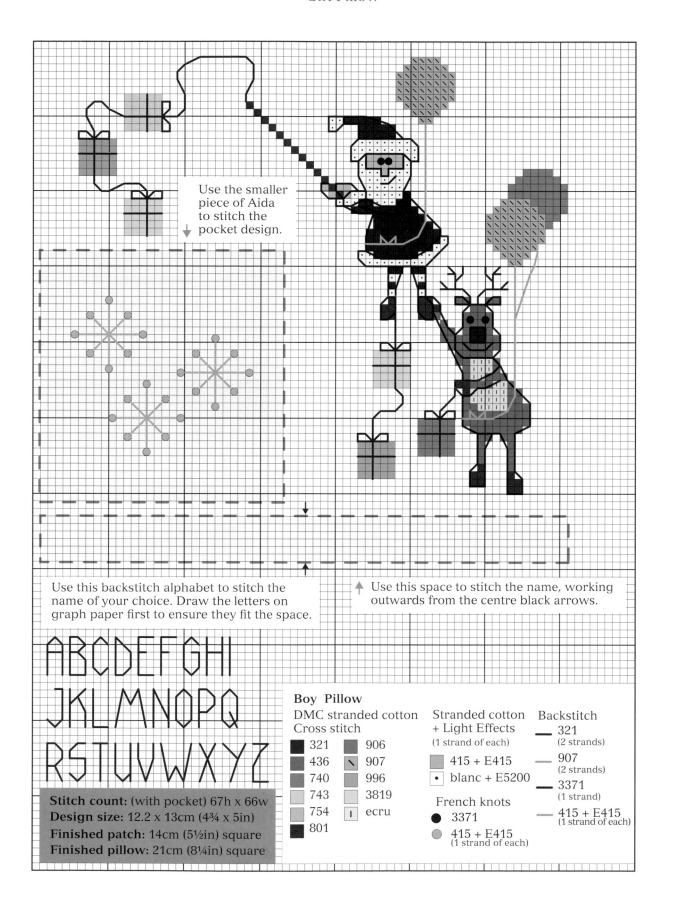

Use the smaller piece of Aida to stitch the pocket design.

Use this backstitch alphabet to stitch the name of your choice. Draw the letters on graph paper first to ensure they fit the space.

⬆ Use this space to stitch the name, working outwards from the centre black arrows.

ABCDEFGHI
JKLMNOPQ
RSTUVWXYZ

Boy Pillow

DMC stranded cotton Cross stitch	Stranded cotton + Light Effects (1 strand of each)	Backstitch
■ 321	■ 906	— 321 (2 strands)
■ 436	\ 907	— 907 (2 strands)
■ 740	■ 996	— 3371 (1 strand)
■ 743	■ 3819	— 415 + E415 (1 strand of each)
■ 754	I ecru	
■ 801		

Stranded cotton + Light Effects (1 strand of each)
■ 415 + E415
• blanc + E5200

French knots
● 3371
● 415 + E415 (1 strand of each)

Stitch count: (with pocket) 67h x 66w
Design size: 12.2 x 13cm (4¾ x 5in)
Finished patch: 14cm (5½in) square
Finished pillow: 21cm (8¼in) square

Happy Holidays

C hristmas is a world-wide occasion and the fun designs in this chapter acknowledge that many people spend it in brilliant sunshine, with barbecues on the beach instead of mulled wine by the fire while snow falls outside. These motifs can be made a little smaller by working them on 16-count Aida instead of 14-count. Refer to page 94 for calculating stitch counts and design sizes.

DESIGNED BY CLAIRE CROMPTON

YOU WILL NEED
(FOR ONE COASTER)

Pale blue 14-count Aida 11.5cm (4½in) square

✻

Tapestry needle size 24

✻

DMC stranded cotton (floss) as listed in chart key

✻

Medium-weight iron-on interfacing

✻

Coaster with a 7.6cm (3in) square or circular aperture

1 Prepare for work, referring to page 94 if necessary. Start stitching from the centre of the fabric and charted motif (charts overleaf) and work outwards over one Aida block using two strands of stranded cotton for cross stitch and French knots and one strand for backstitch.

2 Fuse iron-on interfacing to the wrong side of the design according to the manufacturer's instructions. Using the back plate of the coaster as a guide, trim the fabric so the design fits into the coaster, making sure the design is central. Insert the design into the coaster and push the back plate into place.

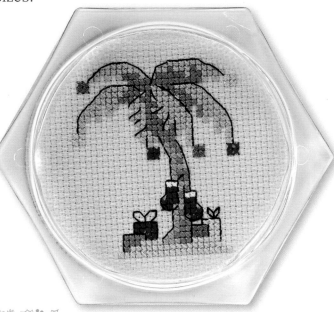

Many of us have friends or relatives living in the southern hemisphere where Christmas is a sunnier event, so these humorous designs are perfect for creating projects just for them. Christmas greetings are charted in Spanish, French, Italian and German, as well as English, so you can personalize the designs. The motifs are just the right size for a range of greetings cards and gift tags. Jazz them up with variegated ribbons and metallic card effects.

DESIGNED BY JANE HENDERSON

YOU WILL NEED

Ready-made oven glove
with cross stitch insert
(DMC – see Suppliers)

❋

Tapestry needle size 24

❋

DMC stranded cotton
(floss) as listed in
chart key

Feathered Friends

Christmas is a time of feasting, with plenty of activity centred on the kitchen and dining room, so why not decorate a range of useful items, such as this fun turkey design on a ready-made oven glove? The charming feathered friends in this chapter would look great on other ready-made items such as recipe books, tablecloths and napkins.

1 Start stitching from the centre of the Aida insert on the glove and from the centre of the charted motif (charts on pages 70–71). Work outwards over one block using two strands of stranded cotton for cross stitch and French knots and one strand for backstitch.

If your oven glove is a store-bought one that doesn't have an Aida insert, then stitch the design on a 12.7cm (5in) square of Aida fabric, hem the edges and sew it to the glove as a patch.

2 Once the embroidery is finished, press the design if required.

Various suppliers have ready-made items with inserts for cross stitch (see Suppliers) allowing you to create a whole range of kitchen and dining room projects using the cute birds charted on pages 70–71. A table runner with some party roosters would be great fun and you could stitch a row of sweet geese on a napkin case. Cooking Christmas dinner is a fine balancing act, so a cheeky robin perched precariously on the top of a tree would be perfect for a cook's apron.

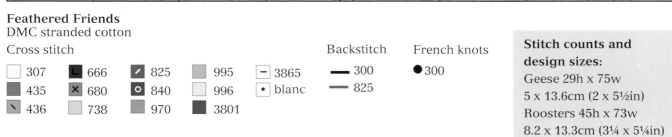

Feathered Friends
DMC stranded cotton

Cross stitch

☐ 307	◪ 666	╱ 825	▨ 995	— 3865	
▨ 435	✕ 680	◉ 840	☐ 996	• blanc	
◥ 436	☐ 738	▨ 970	■ 3801		

Backstitch
— 300
— 825

French knots
● 300

Stitch counts and design sizes:
Geese 29h x 75w
5 x 13.6cm (2 x 5½in)
Roosters 45h x 73w
8.2 x 13.3cm (3¼ x 5¼in)

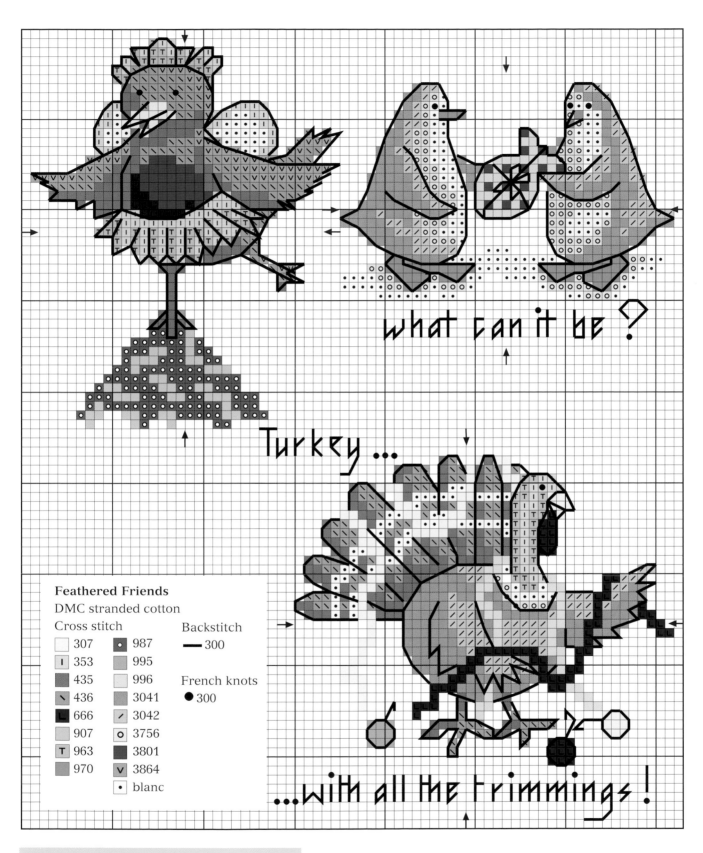

what can it be ?

Turkey ...

...with all the trimmings !

Feathered Friends

DMC stranded cotton

Cross stitch

	307	⊙	987	
I	353		995	
	435		996	
\	436		3041	
◼	666	⁄	3042	
	907	○	3756	
T	963		3801	
	970	V	3864	
		•	blanc	

Backstitch
—— 300

French knots
● 300

Stitch counts and design sizes:

Robin 43h x 34w   7.6 x 6.3cm (3 x 2½in)
Penguins 28h x 37w   5 x 7cm (2 x 2¾in)
Turkey 43h x 46w   7.6 x 8.3cm (3 x 3¼in)

DESIGNED BY JOANNE SANDERSON

YOU WILL NEED
(FOR ONE BAG)

White 14-count Aida
13cm (5in) square

❈

Tapestry needle size 24

❈

DMC stranded cotton
(floss) as in chart key

❈

Iron-on interfacing
13cm (5in) square

❈

Felt 30 x 15cm (12 x 6in) in
a colour to tone with the
embroidery

❈

Velvet ribbon 1.3cm (½in)
wide x 50cm (20in) long,
for handle

❈

Matching sewing thread

Felt So Festive

These cute felt bags are simple to stitch and make up and are perfect for seasonal keepsakes and Christmas gifts. There are four Christmas friends and four winter friends, all in an attractive contemporary style and bold colours. For extra sparkle you could stitch the designs on Lurex Aida. Stitch counts and design sizes are on the chart pages overleaf.

1 Prepare for work, referring to page 94 if necessary. Start stitching from the centre of the fabric and charted motif and work outwards over one Aida block using two strands of stranded cotton for cross stitch and French knots and one strand for backstitch.

2 Once all stitching is complete, fuse iron-on interfacing to the back of the stitching according to the manufacturer's instructions. Trim the embroidered patch to within six Aida blocks of the backstitch square edge on all four sides.

3 Make up as a bag as follows. Fold the piece of felt in half, right sides facing so that the folded edge is at the bottom. Stitch up each side, using a 1cm (³/₈in) seam. Turn the bag the right way out. Use small stitches and matching sewing thread to stitch the embroidered patch to the bag.

4 Cut the ribbon in half to make two handles, and using matching thread, stitch each length of ribbon to the inside of the bag – one on the front piece of felt, the other on the back piece.

The eight fun designs in this chapter would also be ideal for a contemporary set of Christmas cards mounted on single-fold cards and decorated with festive paper and embellishments. Felt is also available with sparkly effects, which would be perfect for a bag for a little girl. You could also glue one of the cross stitch designs to sparkly felt and stiff card to make a picture.

Christmas Friends
DMC stranded cotton

Cross stitch

■ 310	◣ 498	− 738	↘ 800	
▦ 318	■ 608	T 740	948	
V 351	■ 666	743	3706	
O 353	■ 700	L 745	3840	
433	704	762	• B5200	
435	I 712	■ 796		

Backstitch
— 310

French knots
○ B5200

Stitch counts (each design):
38h x 39w max
Design sizes:
6.9 x 6.9cm (2¾ x 2¾in) max

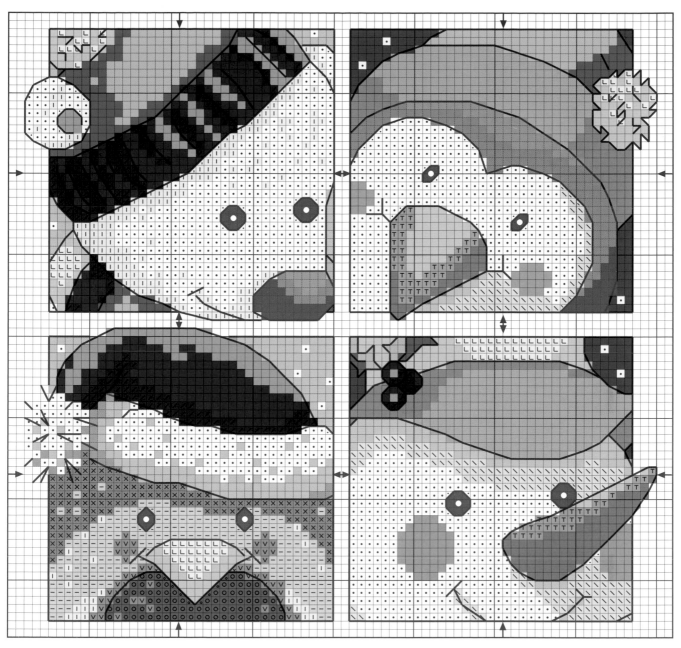

Winter Friends
DMC stranded cotton

Cross stitch

209	413	704	796
211	× 435	I 712	↘ 800
310	╱ 498	725	3706
318	608	– 738	3840
O 350	666	T 740	• B5200
V 352	700	L 745	

Backstitch
— 310

French knots
○ B5200

Stitch counts (each design):
36h x 38w max
Design sizes:
6.5 x 6.9cm (2½ x 2¾in)

DESIGNED BY URSULA MICHAEL

YOU WILL NEED

Two 25.4cm (10in) squares
of gold/white metallic
20-count Lugana (Zweigart
code 3256/018/55)
❄
Tapestry needle size 26
❄
DMC stranded cotton
(floss) as listed in chart key
❄
Two pieces of blue batik
fabric each 31.8 x 76.2cm
(12½ x 30in)
❄
Wadding (batting)
30.5 x 76.2cm (12 x 30in)
❄
White pompom trim
183cm (72in) long
❄
White braid trim
66cm (26in) length
for each snowman
❄
Two 18cm (7in) diameter
circles of fusible
adhesive (such as
Heat'n'Bond Ultrahold)
❄
Tacky glue (optional)

Snow Much Fun!

The eight cheerful snowmen in this chapter will bring a smile to your face on dark and cold winter days and remind you how much fun snow can be. In their brightly coloured clothes and bearing lots of gifts they can be used on a wide variety of projects, such as this seasonal table mat with a fun snowball edging. The finished size of the table mat is 30.5 x 76.2cm (12 x 30in) but could be made longer. You could also sew the snowmen circles on to a ready-made runner.

1 Prepare for work, referring to page 94 if necessary. Start stitching from the centre of the fabric and charted motif (charts overleaf) and work outwards over two fabric threads using three strands of stranded cotton for cross stitch and one for backstitch.

2 Apply fusible adhesive sheets to the back of both embroideries following the manufacturer's instructions. Draw an 18cm (7in) diameter circle in pencil on the backs of the fused stitching, with the embroidery in the centre. Cut on the line, remove the paper backing from the fusible adhesive sheet and make up the table mat as described on page 100.

These cute snowmen are such fun and can be used in many ways – perhaps to decorate individual place mats or napkins, or as circular ornaments for the Christmas tree. All eight snowmen stitched in a long line would make a wonderful table runner for a Christmas buffet table.

These individual snowmen
are perfect for a set of
Christmas cards. Choose
circular-aperture double-
fold cards, perhaps in
a glittery or hammered
finish, and decorate with
seasonal charms and
embellishments.

LESLEY TEARE

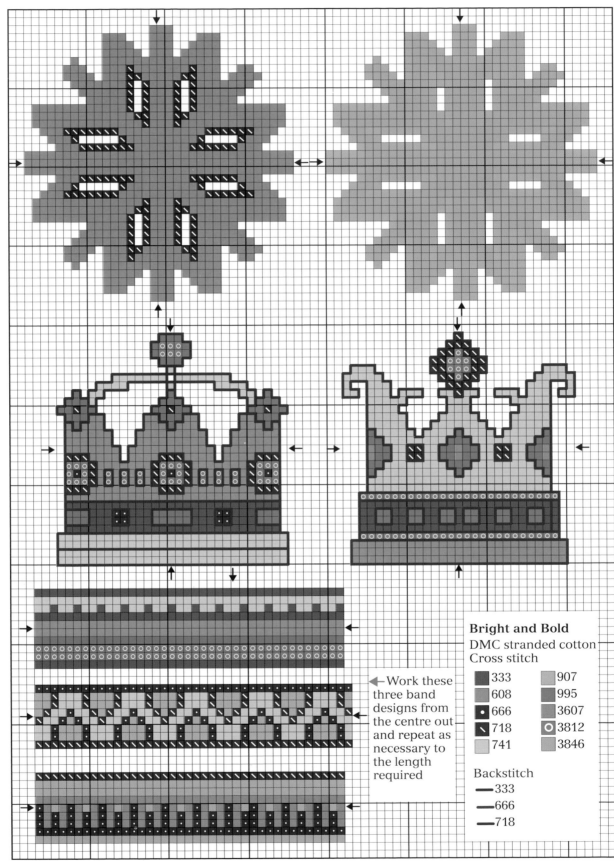

Bright and Bold
DMC stranded cotton
Cross stitch

333	907
608	995
666	3607
718	3812
741	3846

Backstitch
— 333
— 666
— 718

←Work these three band designs from the centre out and repeat as necessary to the length required

Stitch counts and design sizes:
Stars (each) 35h x 34w   6.3 x 6.3cm (2½ x 2½in)
Crowns (each) 29h x 29w   5 x 5cm (2 x 2in)

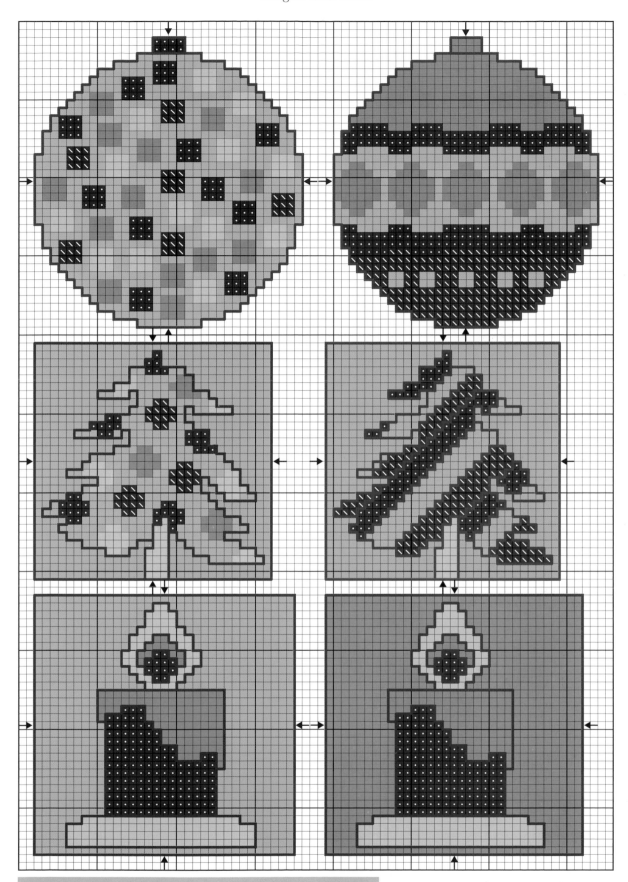

Stitch counts and design sizes:
Baubles (each) 37h x 34w   6.8 x 6.3cm (2¾ x 2½in)
Trees (each) 30h x 30w   5.5 x 5.5cm (2¼ x 2¼in)
Candles (each) 33h x 33w   6 x 6cm (2⅜ x 2⅜in)

JOANNE SANDERSON

Santa please don't forget me

1234567890 ABCDEFGHIJKLMNOPQRSTUVWXYZ

Baby's First Christmas
DMC stranded cotton

Cross stitch

+ 168	701	⁄ 800	995	
\ 310	703	◕ 816	996	
434	725	I 818	948	
∧ 435	L 739	948		
437	\ 744	962	× 3839	
666	745	− 963	• B5200	

437 | 744 | 962 | 3706 |
| | L 739 | 948 | o 3756 |

Backstitch
— 310
— 816
— 938

French knots
● 310

Stitch count for door hanger:
72h x 72w
Design size:
13 x 13cm (5⅛ x 5⅛in)
To work out stitch counts and
design sizes for the other motifs
see page 94

DESIGNED BY CLAIRE CROMPTON

Christmas Stocking

This delightful Christmas stocking is fun to stitch and easy to make up. The bold colours might suit the little boy in your life or you could use pastel shades and the chart on page 89 for a little girl, as shown below. Some parts of the stocking are given an extra festive sparkle by the use of DMC Light Effects threads tweeded with the stranded cotton. The finished stocking is 28.5 x 20.5cm (11¼ x 8in). Refer to the charts for the individual stitch counts and finished design.

1 From the charts overleaf, choose three of the four larger motifs to stitch. For each patch, mark the centre of the Aida piece and the centre of the motif. Start stitching from the centre of the chart and fabric.

2 Stitch the three large motifs working over one Aida block. Use two strands of stranded cotton for cross stitch and French knots. Where stranded cotton and Light Effects thread are used together, use one strand of each. For backstitch use the number of strands indicated in the chart key.

3 Backstitch 'For my small presents' on to the Aida band using two strands of red stranded cotton, making sure the words are centralized on the band.

4 Stitch the four small present motifs on to the remaining square of Aida, making sure that there is plenty of space between them.

5 Once all stitching is complete, refer to page 101 for making up. A template of the stocking is provided on page 102.

YOU WILL NEED

White 14-count Aida: three 15cm (6in) squares for the large motif patches and one 15cm (6in) square for the small presents

❈

White Aida band 5cm (2in) wide (26 stitches) x 16cm (6½in) long

❈

Tapestry needle size 24

❈

DMC stranded cotton (floss) and Light Effects thread as listed in chart key

❈

Felt for stocking 30 x 45cm (12 x 18in)

❈

Lightweight iron-on interfacing in the same sizes as the Aida pieces

❈

Ribbon 15cm (6in) long for a hanging loop

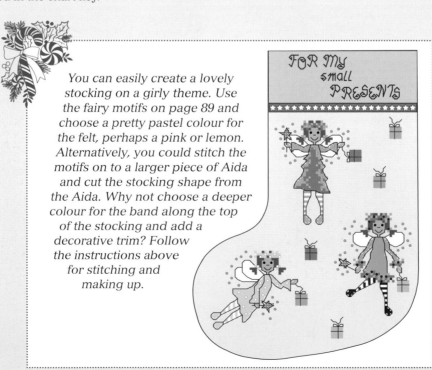

You can easily create a lovely stocking on a girly theme. Use the fairy motifs on page 89 and choose a pretty pastel colour for the felt, perhaps a pink or lemon. Alternatively, you could stitch the motifs on to a larger piece of Aida and cut the stocking shape from the Aida. Why not choose a deeper colour for the band along the top of the stocking and add a decorative trim? Follow the instructions above for stitching and making up.

DESIGNED BY JOAN ELLIOTT

The Nativity

Long ago in a desert land, the heavens guided the way to a humble stable where kings gathered, shepherds bowed and angels sang of the birth of the baby Jesus. Stitched on a light blue evenweave with jewel-toned threads and shimmering metallics, this design will bring the true meaning of Christmas home to everyone and delivers a heartfelt wish for Peace on Earth.

YOU WILL NEED

Light blue 28-count
Jobelan evenweave
33 x 40.5cm (13 x 16in)

❋

Tapestry needle size 24
DMC stranded cotton
(floss) as listed in
chart key

❋

Kreinik #4 Fine Braid
028 citron

❋

Thin wadding (batting)

❋

Double-sided
adhesive tape

❋

Suitable picture frame

1 Prepare for work, referring to page 94 if necessary. Start stitching from the centre of the fabric and the chart overleaf and work outwards over two threads of the fabric.

2 Use two strands of stranded cotton (floss) for cross stitches. Use one strand for Kreinik #4 braid cross stitches and backstitches. Use two strands of DMC 333 for backstitch lettering. Work other backstitches with one strand. Following the chart for the colours, work French knots using one strand wrapped twice around the needle.

3 Once all the stitching is complete, mount the design and frame as a picture (see page 96) or make up in some other way of your choice.

Some motifs from the Nativity design, particularly the kings and shepherds, could be stitched individually for beautiful Christmas cards or a little framed picture, as shown here. You could add a stick-on message or greeting.

Joan Elliott

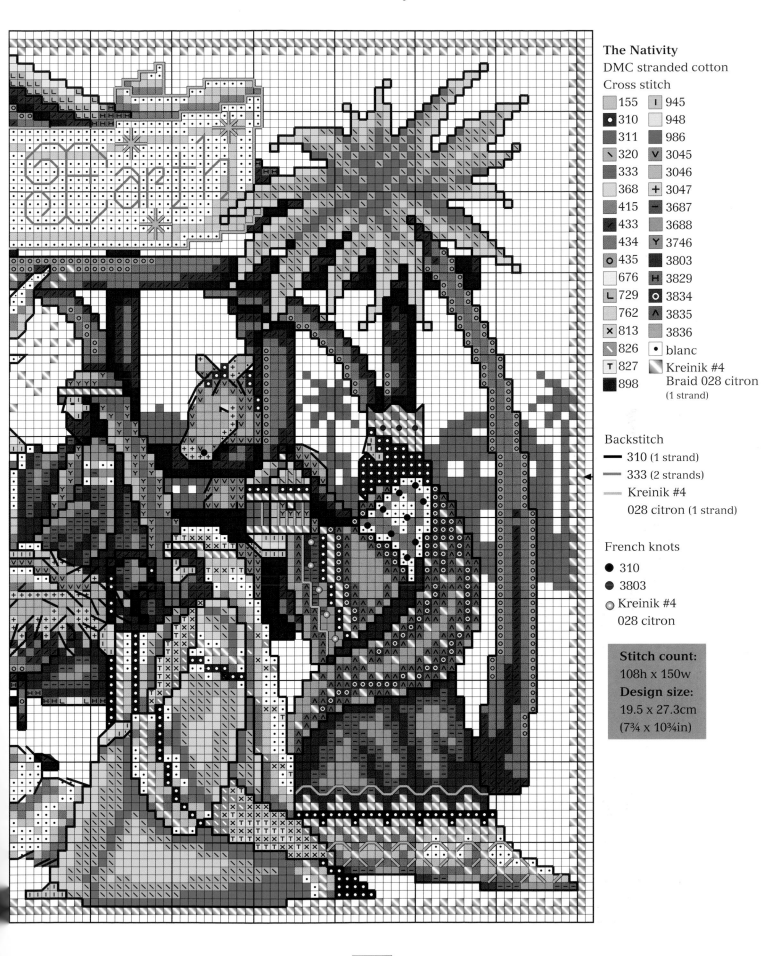

The Nativity
DMC stranded cotton
Cross stitch

155	I	945
310		948
311		986
320	V	3045
333		3046
368	+	3047
415	−	3687
433		3688
434	Y	3746
O 435		3803
676	H	3829
L 729	O	3834
762	Λ	3835
X 813		3836
826	•	blanc
T 827		Kreinik #4
898		Braid 028 citron
		(1 strand)

Backstitch

—— 310 (1 strand)
—— 333 (2 strands)
—— Kreinik #4
    028 citron (1 strand)

French knots

● 310
● 3803
◉ Kreinik #4
    028 citron

Stitch count:
108h x 150w
Design size:
19.5 x 27.3cm
(7¾ x 10¾in)

Materials, Techniques and Stitches

This section is useful to beginners as it describes the materials and equipment required and the basic techniques and stitches needed to work the projects.

Materials

Fabrics

The designs have been worked predominantly on a blockweave fabric called Aida. If you change the gauge (count) of the material, that is the number of holes per inch, then the size of the finished work will alter accordingly. Some of the designs have been stitched on linen evenweave and in this case need to be worked over two fabric threads instead of one block.

Threads

The projects have been stitched with DMC stranded embroidery cotton (floss) but you could match the colours to other thread ranges – ask at your local needlework store. The six-stranded skeins can easily be split into separate threads. The project instructions tell you how many strands to use. Some projects use metallic threads for added glitter.

Embellishments

Many of the projects use embellishments for extra Christmas sparkle: these include beads, charms, ribbons and decorative card and paper. Your local craft store should have a wide range, with many Christmas-themed items.

Needles

Tapestry needles, available in different sizes, are used for cross stitch as they have a rounded point and do not snag fabric. A thinner beading needle will be needed to attach seed beads.

Scissors

You will need a pair of dressmaking shears for cutting fabrics and a small pair of sharp-pointed embroidery scissors for cutting and trimming threads.

Frames

It is a matter of personal preference as to whether you use an embroidery frame or hoop to keep your fabric taut while stitching. Generally, working with a frame helps to keep the tension even and prevent distortion, while working without a frame is faster and less cumbersome. Look in your local needlework store for examples.

Techniques

Preparing the Fabric

❋ Before starting work, check the design size given with each project and make sure that this is the size you require for your finished embroidery. Your fabric must be larger than the finished design size to allow for making up, so allow 13cm (5in) to both dimensions when stitching a picture and 7.5cm (3in) for smaller projects.

❋ Before beginning to stitch, neaten the fabric edges either by hemming or zigzagging to prevent fraying as you work. If using plastic canvas, neaten all the edges by trimming off any rough pieces.

❋ Find the centre of the fabric: this is important regardless of which direction you work from, in order to stitch the design centrally on the fabric. To find the centre, fold the fabric in half horizontally and then vertically, then tack (baste) along the folds (or use tailor's chalk). The centre point is where the two lines cross. This point on the fabric should correspond to the centre point on the chart. Remove these lines on completion of the work.

Calculating Design Size

Each project gives the stitch count and finished design size but if you want to work the design on a different count fabric you will need to re-calculate the finished size. To do this, count the stitches in the height of the design and then the width – this is the stitch count (don't forget to count any backstitches or French knots at the edges). Now divide each of these numbers by the fabric count number. For example, a design with a stitch count of 140 stitches high x 140 stitches wide ÷ 14-count = a finished design size of 10 x 10in (25.5 x 25.5cm). Working on evenweave usually means working over two threads, so divide the fabric count by two before you start calculating.

Using Charts and Keys

The charts in this book are easy to work from. Each square on the chart represents one stitch. Each coloured square, or coloured square with a symbol, represents a thread colour, with the code number given in the chart key. Some designs use three-quarter stitches to give more definition to the design. Solid coloured lines show where backstitches or long stitches are to be worked. French knots are shown by small coloured circles. Beads are shown by larger coloured circles.

Most of the motifs have arrows at the sides to show the centre point, which you could mark. For your own use, you could colour photocopy and enlarge charts.

Starting and Finishing Stitching

It is best to start and finish work correctly, to create the neatest effect and avoid ugly bumps and threads trailing across the back of work. To finish off thread, pass the needle through several nearby stitches on the wrong side of the work, then cut the thread off, close to the fabric.

Knotless Loop Start

Starting this way is useful if you are intending to stitch with an even number of strands, i.e. 2, 4, or 6. Cut the stranded cotton roughly twice the length you would normally need and separate one strand. Double this strand and thread your needle with the two ends. Pierce your fabric from the wrong side where you intend to place your first stitch, leaving the looped end at the back of the work. Return your needle to the wrong side after forming a half cross stitch and pass the needle through the waiting loop. You can now begin to stitch.

Away Waste Knot Start

Start this way if working with an odd number of strands or when tweeding or using variegated threads. Thread your needle and make a knot at the end. Take the needle and thread through from the front of the fabric to the back and come up again about 2.5cm (1in) away from the knot. Now either start cross stitching and work towards the knot, cutting it off when the threads are anchored, or thread the end into your needle and finish off under some completed stitches.

Washing and Pressing

If you need to wash your finished embroidery, first make sure threads are colourfast by washing them in tepid water and mild soap. Rinse well and lay out flat to dry completely before stitching. Wash completed embroideries in the same way. Iron on a medium setting, covering the ironing board with a thick layer of towels. Place stitching right side down and press gently.

Stitches

Backstitch

Backstitches are used to give definition to parts of a design and to outline areas. Many of the charts used different coloured backstitches. Follow the diagram below, bringing the needle up at 1, down at 2, up at 3, down at 4 and so on. On some designs a 'sketchy' backstitch style is used, where the backstitch doesn't always outline the cross stitches exactly.

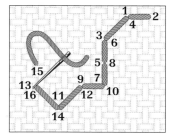

Working backstitch

Blanket Stitch

Blanket stitch is worked in a similar way to buttonhole stitch and has been used to stitch the panels of the Bright and Bold basket together.

Begin with a knotted thread, with the knot hidden inside the project and bring the thread out at the edge of the project where you wish to start. Make a stitch about 6mm (¼in) long (see diagram) and then bring the needle out about 6mm

(¼in) further along, with the working thread under the needle so a loop is formed. Continue all along the line.

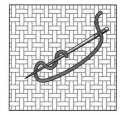

Working blanket stitch

Cross Stitch

A cross stitch can be worked singly over one block of Aida or over two threads of linen or evenweave fabric (see diagrams).

To make a cross stitch over one block of Aida, bring the needle up through the fabric at the bottom right side of the stitch (number 1 on the first diagram) and cross diagonally to 2. Push the needle through the hole and bring it up at 3, crossing the fabric diagonally to 4 to finish the stitch. To work the next stitch, come up through the bottom left corner of the first stitch and repeat the sequence. You can also work cross stitch in two journeys, working a number of half stitches in a line and completing the stitches on the return journey. For neat work, keep all the top stitches facing the same direction.

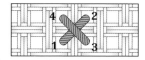

A single cross stitch on Aida

A single cross stitch on evenweave (linen)

Long Stitch

You may use this stitch occasionally, for example for flower stamens or stars. Simply work a long, straight stitch starting and finishing at the points indicated on the chart.

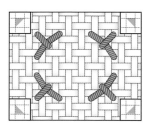

Working long stitch

French Knot

French knots have been used as highlights and details in some of the designs, in various colours. To work, follow the diagram below, bringing the needle and thread up through the fabric at the exact place where the knot is to be positioned. Wrap the thread once around the needle (or according to the project instructions), holding the thread firmly close to the needle, then twist the needle back through the fabric close to where it first emerged. Holding the knot down carefully, pull the thread through to the back leaving the knot on the surface, securing it with one small stitch on the back.

Working a French knot

Three-quarter Cross Stitch

Three-quarter cross stitches give more detail to a design. They are shown by a triangle within a square on the charts. Working three-quarter cross stitches is easier on evenweave fabric than Aida (see diagram below). To work on Aida, work a half cross stitch across the diagonal and then make make a quarter stitch from the corner into the centre of the Aida square, piercing the fabric.

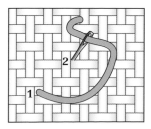

Working three-quarter cross stitch

Attaching Beads

Beads can bring sparkle and texture to your cross stitch embroidery. Attach seed beads using ordinary sewing thread that matches the fabric colour and a beading needle or very fine 'sharp' needle and a half or whole cross stitch.

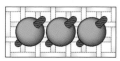

Attaching beads

Making Up

The projects in this book have been made up in a wide variety of lovely ways to give you plenty of ideas on using the charted designs. See Suppliers for useful addresses.

Mounting and Framing Embroidery

1 Cut a piece of acid-free mount board to fit the frame aperture (draw around the frame's backing board). Using double-sided tape, stick a piece of wadding (batting) to the mount board and trim the wadding to the same size.

2 Lay the embroidery right side up on to the wadding, making sure the design is central and straight. Push pins through at the four corners and along the edges to mark the position. Trim the fabric to leave 5cm (2in) all around.

3 Turn the embroidery and mount board over together. Stick double-sided tape around the edges of the board to a depth of 5cm (2in) and peel off the backing. Fold the excess fabric back, pressing down firmly to stick the fabric to the board, adding more tape to neaten the corners. Remove the pins and reassemble the frame with the embroidery in it. It is not necessary to use the glass, as this often flattens the stitches.

Using Ready-made Items

There are many ready-made items specially made for displaying embroidery, including notebooks, coasters, key rings, baby bibs and kitchen items. Mount your work into these items following the manufacturer's instructions. Use a piece of paper or thin card to hide the back of any stitching that may be seen. You could back the stitched design with iron-on interfacing to add stiffness and prevent fabric fraying – see opposite.

Mounting Work into Cards

Many of the designs or parts of larger designs can be stitched and made up into cards and there are many styles of card mounts available today. Some are simple single-fold cards as seen here, while others are pre-folded with three sections, the middle one having a window for the embroidery.

1 To mount embroidery in a ready-made double-fold card, position the embroidery in the window space – the fabric should be at least 2.5cm (1in) larger than the aperture all round. Place strips of double-sided adhesive tape on the card to secure the embroidery (some cards already have this in place).

2 Peel the backing from the tape and fold over the third of the card to cover. This can also be secured with tape for a neater finish. For a personal touch embellish with ribbons, bows, buttons or charms.

Using Iron-on Interfacing and Adhesive Webbing

Iron-on interfacing can be used to stiffen and stabilize your cross stitch embroidery and allow the edges to be cut without fraying. Adhesive webbing is available as single-sided and double-sided, i.e., with glue on one side or both, allowing you to fuse the embroidery to another fabric. This means that you can use your cross stitch to decorate all sorts of ready-made items. Cut the interfacing or webbing to size and fuse it to the back of the finished embroidery with a medium iron, placing the embroidery face down into some thick towels.

Making up the Advent Calendar

1 Once all the stitching is complete, trim each motif ten rows beyond the square and fold along this line of stitches. Finger press in place, mitring the corners. To create hangers cut twenty-four 8.9cm (3½in) lengths of Kreinik ribbon and one 13.9cm (5½in) length for motif 25.

2 With wrong sides together (right sides out), use two strands of matching stranded cotton to whip stitch the running backstitches from corresponding picture and number motifs, starting at centre bottom. As you go add a bead to every other stitch using gold beads for the DMC 729 squares; green beads for the DMC 700 squares and red beads for the DMC 349 squares. For motif 25, use all three beads, alternating colours as you go. At the top edge, insert the ends of the ribbon at each side, securing with whip stitching to create a hanger. Before finishing, stuff with a little polyester filling and finish whip stitching.

3 Make up into a banner as follows. Cut two 53.3 x 38cm (21 x 15in) pieces of background fabric plus three 15 x 10cm (6 x 4in) pieces for tabs. Cut four 5 x 38cm (2 x 15in) pieces of edging fabric and four 5 x 63.5cm (2 x 25in) pieces.

4 Using a 1.3cm (½in) seam and with wrong sides together, sew the shorter lengths of edging fabric to the top and bottom of each piece of background fabric. Press seams open. Using a 1.3cm (½in) seam, with wrong sides together, sew the longer lengths of edging fabric to the long sides of the background fabric. Cut a 63.5 x 43cm (25 x 17in) piece of fusible fleece and fuse this to the wrong side of one of the completed background fabric pieces.

5 To make the tabs, fold each 15 x 10cm (6 x 4in) piece in half lengthwise, right sides together. Sew a 1.3cm (½in) seam down the length and across one short end. Trim the seam, turn right side out and press. Place the two pieces of background fabric right sides facing and pin the tabs evenly across the top with sewn ends pointing towards the centre and raw edges matching (tabs inside the layers at this point). Stitch a 1.3cm (½in) seam all round leaving a gap at the bottom. Turn right side out, press and slipstitch the gap.

6 Bring the loose ends of the tabs to the front and attach to the banner by sewing on large star buttons. Insert the dowel through the tabs. Using the photograph of the banner as a guide, attach each pillow using the small star buttons as hangers.

Making up the Scandinavian Cone

1 Cut the cone shape out along your pencil line. Fold the shape with long, straight edges together (right sides together) and join with a narrow seam. Turn the cone to the right side.

2 Cut a 23cm (9in) length of bias binding. Carefully apply permanent fabric glue to the outside top edge of the cone and glue the binding in place all round. Allow to dry. Apply more glue to the inside top edge of the cone, fold the binding over and press into place to cover the raw edge. Trim any excess.

3 To make a handle, cut a 23cm (9in) length of bias binding, fold it in half lengthways and glue together. Place the ends inside the cone at either side and slipstitch in place.

Making up the Scandinavian Heart

1 Once all the stitching is complete, trace and cut out the heart template on page 13. Position the template centrally on your embroidery, mark the outline in pencil on your fabric and cut out the shape. Cut another heart shape from the other piece of Aida (or use a Christmas print fabric).

2 Place the two shapes right sides together and stitch together all round leaving an opening at the top for turning through. Stuff with a little polyester stuffing or some scented pot-pourri. Insert a ribbon hanging loop into the gap at the top and slipstitch the gap closed. Add a bow to finish.

Making up a Winter Sachet

1 Trim the completed embroidery to the required size and cut a matching piece of backing fabric. With the right sides facing, stitch the two pieces together, leaving the top open for turning through. Turn through to the right side and stuff with pot-pourri or polyester stuffing.

2 For a flower design, make a loop of gold ribbon and place the ends into the top right corner and slipstitch the gap closed. This sachet will then hang on point. For a bird design, which hangs straight, attach the ribbon ends at each top corner and then slipstitch the gap closed.

3 To finish a flower sachet, sew a tassel to the bottom point of the sachet. For a bird sachet, sew a small bell in each base corner.

Making up Santa's Post Bag

1 Cut a piece of fusible fleece 2.5cm (1in) larger than the finished embroidery all round. Centre over the wrong side of the embroidery and fuse together. Trim the prepared embroidery to fourteen rows beyond the design. Fold the top edge back by seven rows and press in place.

2 Cut three 30.5 x 38cm (12 x 15in) pieces of fabric for the lining and backing. Fold one piece to match the size of the trimmed embroidery. Place this right sides together with the embroidery, matching folded edges, and stitch along the sides and bottom using a 1.3cm (½in) seam. Turn to the right side and slipstitch the folded edges closed.

3 Cut a 30.5 x 38cm (12 x 15in) piece of interfacing and fuse to the wrong side of one of the remaining fabric pieces. Place the two pieces of fabric together, wrong sides facing and stitch a 1.3cm (½in) seam all round leaving at gap at bottom for turning. Turn right side out and slipstitch the gap closed.

4 Place the prepared embroidery right side up on top of the backing and slipstitch the sides and bottom edges together. Cut two 15.2cm (6in) pieces of trim and starting from the top front of the backing, glue in place 2.5cm (1in) from either side edge. Turn the top edge back by 5cm (2in) to form a casing. Stitch a line 3.8cm (1½in) from the folded edge and another row 6mm (¼in) below that.

5 Glue the trim around the finished embroidery starting and ending at centre bottom, attaching a button where the ends meet. Attach the remaining buttons along the trim on the backing fabric referring to the photo for positions. Fold back the ends of the remaining trim to form loops and glue in place. Insert the dowel through the casing and looped ends of the trim.

Making up a Mantel Stocking

1 Cut a piece of iron-on interfacing 4.5 x 17.7cm (1¾ x 7in) and fuse it to the back of the finished embroidery. Cut two pieces of iron-on interfacing the size of the patterned fabric pieces and fuse to the back of each piece.

2 Trace and cut out the stocking template on page 29, and with wrong sides facing, cut the fabric to the stocking shape. Position the finished embroidery on the right side of one piece of fabric with the toe facing left and 6.4cm (2½in) from the top edge. Place the second piece of fabric on top, right sides facing and stitch a 1.3cm (½in) seam all around leaving the top of the stocking open and a gap at the bottom for tucking in the ends of the decorative trim. Trim the seams and turn right side out. Fold the top edges in by 5cm (2in) and press.

3 Attach the bells to the bottom edge of the Aida band. Fold the length of ribbon in half and attach with a few small stitches to the inside right corner to form a hanging loop. Using permanent fabric glue, attach the decorative trim starting and ending at the bottom gap. Slipstitch the gap closed.

Making up the Mitten Garland

1 Once all stitching is complete, draw a pencil line on the back of all of the mittens 6mm (¼in) out from the stitching all round. Place a mitten right side together with a piece of backing fabric and pin together. Sew around the mitten along the pencil line, leaving an opening for turning. Trim excess fabric. Turn through to the right side, fill with stuffing and sew the opening closed. Repeat for the other mittens.

2 Cut four 30.5cm (12in) lengths of silver ribbon. Make four bows and sew a bow to the top of each mitten. Arrange the mittens in a vertical garland with the thumbs facing left, then right, left, then right. Sew two silver bells to the front of each bow. Now stitch the mittens together.

3 Make a hanger by folding a length of silver ribbon in half and sewing it to the top of the garland. If desired, sew a large bow made from wider blue ribbon to the top of the garland.

Making up a Beaded Decoration

1 Trim the stitched decoration to five Aida blocks from the outline of the design all round. Cut a piece of backing fabric to the same size. Place the two pieces right sides together and using a 6mm (¼in) seam, stitch together along three sides.

2 Trim the seams to within two blocks of the seam lines, trim across corners and turn through to the right side, pushing the corners out carefully. Cut two squares of wadding (batting) to the size of the decoration and slip them inside, pushing them into the corners. Fold the remaining raw edges of the fabric inwards and using matching thread slipstitch the edges neatly together to close the square. Tuck a loop of narrow gold ribbon into the gap as you close it. Using the same colour thread, stitch seed beads around the edges of the square, positioning one on each corner.

3 For a bead tassel, choose a selection of mixed beads to add to the bottom corner (or three corners if desired). Secure a length of thread near the corner seed bead and then add your beads to the needle, finishing with a larger bead (or a large sequin) and a seed bead. Skipping the last seed bead added, take the needle and thread back up the row of beads and fasten off the thread.

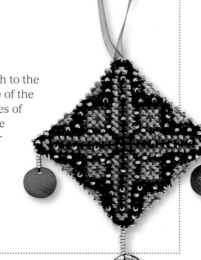

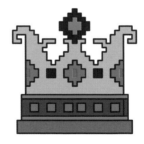

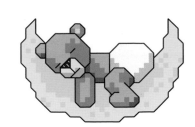
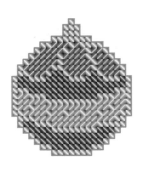